I0031872

Progressives on the Hudson

Progressives on the Hudson

Their Impact on
New York State Politics and Policy

MICHAEL A. ARMATO

ee

excelsior editions

State University of New York Press
Albany, New York

Cover photo taken in Esopus by Michael Armato.

Published by State University of New York Press, Albany

© 2025 State University of New York

All rights reserved

Printed in the United States of America

No part of this book may be used or reproduced in any manner whatsoever without written permission. No part of this book may be stored in a retrieval system or transmitted in any form or by any means including electronic, electrostatic, magnetic tape, mechanical, photocopying, recording, or otherwise without the prior permission in writing of the publisher.

Links to third-party websites are provided as a convenience and for informational purposes only. They do not constitute an endorsement or an approval of any of the products, services, or opinions of the organization, companies, or individuals. SUNY Press bears no responsibility for the accuracy, legality, or content of a URL, the external website, or for that of subsequent websites.

EU GPSR Authorised Representative:
Logos Europe, 9 rue Nicolas Poussin, 17000, La Rochelle, France
contact@logoseurope.eu

Excelsior Editions is an imprint of State University of New York Press

For information, contact State University of New York Press, Albany, NY
www.sunypress.edu

Library of Congress Cataloging-in-Publication Data

Name: Armato, Michael A., 1984– author.
Title: Progressives on the Hudson : their impact on New York State politics
    and policy / Michael A. Armato.
Description: Albany : State University of New York Press, [2025]. | Includes
    bibliographical references and index.
Identifiers: LCCN 2024044576 | ISBN 9798855802528 (hardcover : alk. paper) |
    ISBN 9798855802542 (ebook) | ISBN 9798855802535 (pbk. : alk. paper)
Subjects: LCSH: Political participation—Hudson River Valley (N.Y. and N.J.) |
    Political activists—Hudson River Valley (N.Y. and N.J.) | Local government—
    Hudson River Valley (N.Y. and N.J.) | Progressivism (United States politics)—
    Hudson River Valley (N.Y. and N.J.) | Hudson River Valley (N.Y. and N.J.)—
    Politics and government. | New York (State)—Politics and government.
Classification: LCC JS451.N79 H843 2025 | DDC 324.2732/7—dc23/eng/20250212
LC record available at https://lccn.loc.gov/2024044576

For Gina

If you drop a rose in the Hudson River at its mysterious source in the Adirondacks, think of all the places it journeys by as it goes out to sea forever—think of that wonderful Hudson Valley.

—Jack Kerouac, *On the Road*

Contents

Acknowledgments

I can never repay the multitude of individuals who helped make this project a reality. First, my sincerest thanks to my family. My wife, Dr. Gina Watzka, to whom this work is dedicated, can never be repaid for her support of this endeavor. From our undergraduate days at Wagner College, through graduate school, through tenure, through this work—she has been a steadfast and patient supporter of my journey in academia. And these words are simply not enough to truly describe her support. Truth be told, Gina, an Ulster County native, is the person who introduced me to the magnificent Hudson Valley. So, in a sense, I owe this all to her. I also am grateful to my parents, Marc and Anna Armato, for supporting my career and education, and for encouraging me for as long as I can remember. Special thanks to my mother- and father-in-law, Edward and Denise Watzka, also Hudson Valley natives, for providing the gift of childcare while I traversed the Hudson Valley listening to the stories of progressive activists.

Dr. Michael Rinella is the reason I undertook this project at all. He has been generous and patient. And I sincerely thank him for all of his contributions to the scholarship of the Empire State. Dr. Lisa Parshall of Daemen University also deserves special appreciation. Her comments on a very early conference paper, without a doubt, put this project on a successful path. It is not an exaggeration to say that her insights had the biggest substantive impact on this work, and for that I am thankful. Dr. Sally Friedman of the University at Albany, State University of New York, also deserves my sincerest thanks for her guidance and support of this project from the beginning, as does Dr. Julie Novkov, dean of Rockefeller College of Public Affairs and Policy at the University at Albany, for her insights.

Appreciation is given to the peer reviewers who made this work better and provided useful and actionable comments, while also being generous not only in giving their time, but their kindness. And my sincerest thanks for the support I received from my colleagues at Albright College. Dr. Irene Langran and Dr. Nathan Henceroth have been particularly helpful. I also appreciate the support of Dr. Elizabeth Kiester, Dr. Jennifer Koosed, and Dr. Ian Rhile. My thanks is given to Albright's Professional Council for their support, as well as to those in Academic Affairs Administration at Albright. In particular, my sincerest thanks to Leigh Anne Fernandes and Angela Fonte. I am also thankful to Dr. Bridget Hearon and Dr. Laura Gelety for their assistance with protocols. Thank you to Dr. Brian Jennings for assistance with software and to Timothy Kiester for assistance with technology.

Last, but certainly not least, my sincerest and heartiest admiration and thanks to the sixty-four progressive activists who generously dedicated their time to this endeavor. These are the people who make democracy work in the region. I have never met a group whose sense of civic obligation and selflessness inspires me more robustly. I sincerely hope I have done justice to your service to the Hudson Valley. Your civic engagement helped us understand not only politics and policy in the Hudson Valley but also progressive ideology far more broadly. To each and every one of you, my most profound thanks.

Chapter 1

Progressives and the Hudson Valley

Setting the Scene

One of the benefits of living in the Hudson Valley of New York is the opportunity to attend the Ulster County Fair. Corndogs, frozen lemonade, 4-H contests, and miniature pig races are all part of the trappings of the event hosted in the town of New Paltz. Since 2006, I have attended this fair as often as my schedule allowed. While the casual onlooker will see carnival rides and cotton candy, the student of politics cannot help but notice the political and ideological dimensions of the people who frequent this event.

At the 2006 fair, I was asked to sign a nominating petition for the New York State Green Party's slate of candidates. While the effort required to obtain signatures for a party in New York without permanent ballot status is indeed herculean, a small but loyal team of volunteers single-mindedly set about the task of gathering as many signatures as possible.[1] In truth, Ulster County was a rather fertile ground on which to collect signatures for a progressive political party.

Just several years earlier, the Greens held a hotly contested primary election for three state committee seats in the county (Ulster County Board of Elections 2002). Prior to 2020, a political party in New York held permanent ballot status by earning fifty thousand votes in the most recent gubernatorial election. This allowed party enrollees to elect state committee members in taxpayer-organized party primaries. Since the 2020 presidential

---

1. The Green Party enjoyed permanent ballot status in New York from 1999 through the end of 2002. It regained ballot status at the 2010 General Election, which it held through the end of 2020.

election, political parties "must receive the greater of 130,000 votes or two percent of votes cast in the previous presidential or gubernatorial election" in order to be recognized as a qualified party in New York.[2] The major parties elect state committee members from whole or parts of state assembly districts, while other smaller parties elect state committee members either countywide or by congressional district (New York State Board of Elections 2017). While it held ballot status, the Green Party chose its state committee members in countywide primaries (Green Party of New York State 2015).

In total, 378 out of 866 enrolled Green Party members cast ballots countywide for nonpaying party positions in that particular contest (New York State Board of Elections 2002; Ulster County Board of Elections 2002). That is a 43.6 percent turnout, an extremely respectable number in any primary contest. The Ulster County Board of Elections further indicates that 111 of the 378 votes cast came from Greens in the town of New Paltz.

I did not see a booth dedicated to the Green Party ten years later at the 2016 fair. Yet, a noticeable number of attendees donned Teachout for Congress stickers. Zephyr Teachout became somewhat of a progressive heroine in 2014, after running an unsuccessful primary against Governor Andrew Cuomo for the Democratic Party ballot line. While she earned just 34.3 percent of the vote against the incumbent, it was still a remarkable feat, considering how well established Governor Cuomo was in the state political scene (New York State Board of Elections 2014b). Essentially, a person few had heard of outside the halls of academia garnered over one-third of the vote in a nominating contest against one of the nation's political heavyweights at the time.

Teachout's performance in the ten counties that encompass the Hudson Valley was even more impressive (US Election Atlas 2014; New York State Board of Elections 2014d). She won 77.91 percent in Columbia County and 69.95 percent in Ulster. Teachout also broke 60 percent of the vote in Albany, Greene, and Rensselaer Counties, and took 57.51 percent in Dutchess. She won Putnam more narrowly, with 53.55 percent of the vote, and just barely lost Orange with 48.15 percent. Thus, Teachout earned a majority of the primary vote in seven of those counties, many of which are home to urban places, suburban communities, and rural areas.

Further, at the progressive Working Families Party (WFP) state committee meeting that year, Teachout earned the votes of 41 percent of members in their gubernatorial nominating process, even garnering the

---

2. SAM Party v. Kosinski, 483 F. Supp. 3d 245 2020 US Dist.

endorsement of Bertha Lewis, one of the party's founders and a nationally known progressive figure (Nahmias 2014). Additionally, Howie Hawkins, Green Party nominee for governor, earned over 5 percent of the vote in Dutchess and Greene Counties at the 2014 General Election and broke 10 percent in Columbia, Ulster, Albany, and Rensselaer Counties (New York State Board of Elections 2014b). While there was a noticeable distaste among public employees toward then Governor Andrew Cuomo, the fact that such a left-wing candidate garnered these vote totals is further indicative of a progressive presence in these counties.

Then, of course, there was the support for Senator Bernie Sanders in the 2016 Democratic presidential nominating contest. Senator Sanders beat Secretary Clinton in seven of the ten counties that compose the Hudson Valley (*New York Times* 2016; New York State Board of Elections 2016a). More precisely, Sanders won a majority of the vote in Putnam, Dutchess, and Albany Counties. He broke 55 percent of all votes cast in Columbia, Greene, and Rensselaer Counties. And he earned 62.6 percent in Ulster County. Thus, Secretary Clinton lost a number of counties in her own state to a more progressive challenger.

Sanders supporters continued to be active in the local political establishment (Muscavage 2016; Ulster County Board of Elections 2016). Kelleigh McKenzie, a Sanders delegate, won a seat on the Democratic state committee in 2016, earning almost 64 percent of the vote in a contested primary election (Ulster County Board of Elections 2016). Thus, the Sanders campaign ushered in the election of progressive Democratic Party officials in the area.

The area's progressive nature is also chronicled in media sources. Per *The Hudson Valley Post* and *The Daily Freeman*, Crowdpac, which bills itself as a nonpartisan government reform group, via their own measures, ranks the town of Rosendale, a relatively rural community in Ulster County, the third "most liberal" in the nation (Kemble 2015; Welber 2015). New Paltz, Beacon, and Putnam Valley were also ranked in the top 450 liberal cities (Welber 2015). Per Welber, the research was based on a nationwide analysis of party donations per capita in municipalities with over six thousand residents.

Beyond the Crowdpac study, news sources also show us the progressive pulse of the region. For example, the former mayor of New Paltz was arrested in 2004 for marrying twenty-five same-sex couples before doing so was legal in New York (Lueck 2004). More recently, *The Journal News* stated that over 3,400 individuals from the Hudson Valley marched on Washington at the National Women's March (Rom 2016). Further, in 2017, Poughkeepsie was home to a May Day rally that advocated for the city to become a "sanctuary city" (*MidHudson News* 2017). Also, the left-wing Working Families Party employs a regional director in the area (*Daily Freeman* 2017; Working Families Party 2017). Thus, one does not need to delve too far into local news sources to see the pulse of progressivism in the region.

There is also an extensive progressive social media presence. A superficial search of Facebook groups in the area indicates that at least fifteen separate progressive-oriented groups operate in the region. There are also websites connected to many of those Facebook groups, such as the Albany Social Justice Center and the Dutchess County Progressive Action Alliance (DCPAA). Thus, the evidence presented thus far indicates that there is a strong progressive pulse throughout the Hudson Valley.

But beyond what has been presented in the chapter thus far, what do we know about the nature of progressivism in the Hudson Valley? Can it be called a movement in its own right, or is it a series of movements? Are progressives in this region remnants of the Liberal Party of New York, left-leaning Democrats, and members of the Working Families Party? Are they environmentalists, organic farmers, and Green Party enrollees? Are they rich celebrities who film in New York City but retire to the Hudson Valley at the end of the filming week? What role, if any, does the burgeoning arts community in the region play in the story? What overlap is there between different subsets of a larger progressive movement? Is there a progressive identity in the region?

More broadly than simply thinking about this book as solely a work on the Hudson Valley, are progressives only denizens of America's largest cities? How do progressive activists articulate their ideology and civic engagement in areas outside of large metropolises like New York City, San Francisco, and Boston? What can we learn from progressive activists in this region that might help us to understand progressives who live outside of our largest cities in other parts of the nation? And, perhaps most importantly, why should we care about any of these questions?

This work advances three main arguments. First, there is a robust and diverse progressive presence in New York's Hudson Valley. These activists are a visible and important part of the electoral and policymaking arenas, as well as the civic community at large that exists outside of these two important areas. Second, progressives practice their civic engagement in parts of the nation outside of America's largest cities. Simply, progressives are found in areas where the media narrative tells us they should not exist. Thus, scholars of ideology and civic engagement will do well to learn from the narratives of progressive actors in the Hudson Valley, and to explore whether their experiences can be compared to those in other electoral and policymaking theaters outside of the Hudson Valley. How do progressive activists in New York compare to those in the state of Vermont or Door County, Wisconsin, for example? Thus, this work is about the Hudson Valley, but it may have wider applicability to help scholars and students understand progressives living in other parts of the nation outside of America's largest cities like New York and San Francisco. Third, the binding hallmark of progressive ideology is employing government and nonprofits to fight the status quo and advance equity and equal opportunity.

The second chapter of this work will explain the third argument more thoroughly. That said, it is important to make several qualifications before moving forward. Progressives use government in specific ways to achieve their goals. They work diligently to help their preferred candidates win elections. A number of subjects ran for office; a number hold elected office or were appointed to government positions. Progressives also lobby governments to achieve their policy goals. Their efforts bring them before legislators, chief executives, and bureaucratic policymakers at every level of government.

Progressives also use nonprofits to bring about equity and equal opportunity. For the purposes of this work, a nonprofit means any organization that is not a profit-making entity or a government. Nonprofits include political parties, landbanks, advocacy organizations, and any other entity that may qualify under the 501(c), 509, and 527 sections of the federal tax code (Internal Revenue Service 2021). It does not only mean a 501(c) 3 charity. The term *nonprofit* is deliberately used because, as we will see, progressives do not usually have great affection for profit-making entities whom they often battle. That does not mean that progressives believe there is no place for business, especially small business, only that most subjects prefer to use governments or nonprofits as vehicles to achieve their goals. Furthermore, the following pages will illustrate that progressives often use nonprofits as vehicles to lobby government.

Going forward, chapter 2 highlights the diversity of ways that these activists think about their own ideology and the diversity of individuals that compose the overarching progressive movement in the Hudson Valley. Clearly, this can serve as a reference point for progressives in other parts of the nation. Chapter 3 will explore progressives in the electoral arena, and chapter 4 will furnish readers with a rich overview of their policymaking activities. Chapter 5 will illustrate the robust progressive presence in other civic endeavors. Finally, chapter 6 will do two things. First, it will show how progressives create social capital. Second, it will offer concluding thoughts about progressives, their ideology, and their contributions to political and civic life in the Hudson Valley and beyond. But before readers can appreciate those chapters, more needs to be explained about the Hudson Valley, progressive ideology, and the methodology of this work.

To begin, this work adds to the social science literature on the Hudson Valley. One of the clearest pictures of the region is given to us by Sally Friedman (2007) in her work that explores the home-style activities of former US Rep. Maurice Hinchey of Ulster County, US Rep. Sue Kelly of Westchester County, and US Rep. Michael McNulty of Albany County. Friedman presented some of the most detailed characteristics of much of the Hudson Valley to readers that exist in scholarship. Further, Duncan and Duncan (2004) studied land use in the town of Bedford, located in Westchester County. This work provides readers with a lucid description of a part of Westchester County and the politics of land use in the area. In particular, Duncan and Duncan reveal the nature of how micropolitics is leveraged to achieve desirable aesthetic qualities, at least for certain parts of the population. Additionally, Gerald Benjamin (2017) published an article studying the Chassidic presence on municipal affairs in the region. And Armato (2022) explored the organizational, electoral, and policymaking activities of the Liberal Party in the Hudson Valley from 1948 to 1963. This included their efforts to reregister New Yorkers with two homes to vote at their Hudson Valley addresses, something popular with today's progressive activists in the region.

Beyond these notable works, a great deal of scholarship on the Hudson Valley largely relies on scholars of the humanities, such as Robert Lifset, the late David Schuyler, and a host of other academics whose work is published by *The Hudson River Valley Review*. But more work could be done by social scientists.

The US Census Bureau estimates that over 2.9 million residents live in the ten counties that compose the region. To put this number in perspective, the population of the area is larger than that of fifteen states of the union.

Further, the Hudson Valley is home to a number of competitive congressional seats, as redistricted for the 2022 General Election. In particular, the nineteenth congressional district has an even Partisan Voter Index score. The eighteenth congressional district of New York has a Partisan Voter Index rating of D+1. The seventeenth congressional district of New York has a rating of D+3. And Rep. Paul Tonko's district also has a PVI rating below D+10, at D+7, theoretically making it electorally competitive (Cook Political 2023). Further, President Trump won four of the ten counties in the region and lost Dutchess County by less than 1 percent of the vote in 2016 (*New York Times* 2016). In 2020, President Trump won just three counties in the area, but five of those counties were decided by less than ten points. Simply put, the region is electorally competitive (New York State Board of Elections 2020).

Beyond this, Hudson Valley state legislators represent a significant portion of the state assembly and senate. Indeed, over 10 percent of the memberships of both of these chambers are from this region (New York State Legislative Task Force on Demographic Research and Reapportionment). Prior to the 2022 redistricting, we can see just how competitive these districts were electorally.

Seven state senators found their districts entirely within the Hudson Valley and another six represented portions of the region (New York State Legislative Task Force on Demographic Research and Reapportionment). From 2014 to 2020, no winner of the fortieth and forty-first state senate districts, which were entirely within the Hudson Valley, broke 59 percent of the vote at any general election (New York State Board of Elections 2014b, 2016b, 2018, 2020). Over the same time frame, the winners of the thirty-seventh state senate district, entirely within the Hudson Valley, and of the forty-sixth state senate district, partially in the region, won with less than 60 percent of the vote in three out of four elections. At the 2018 General Election, the winners of three districts completely within the region, and an additional three partially within the Hudson Valley, did not break 60 percent of the vote. And, in 2020, the victors in five districts entirely within the Hudson Valley and an additional four partially within the area were elected with less than 60 percent of votes cast. Simply, this region plays an important role in determining the majority of that chamber.

Furthermore, seventeen members of the state assembly represented districts entirely within the region while another six members represented portions of the area (New York State Legislative Task Force on Demographic Research and Reapportionment). From 2014 to 2020, the winners of two seats entirely within the region won with less than 60 percent of the vote in each election, and the winners of three other seats entirely within the Hudson Valley only broke 60 percent of the vote in one cycle (New York State Board of Elections 2014, 2016a, 2018, 2020). The 2018 and 2020 elections are more striking.

In the 2018 election cycle, the winners of nine seats entirely within the Hudson Valley and two whose districts are partially in the borders of the region were elected with less than 60 percent of the vote. Thus, eleven of the seventeen seats were competitive in that cycle (New York State Board of Elections 2018). In 2020, nine members of assembly whose districts are entirely in the Hudson Valley did not break 59 percent, and another member whose district is partially within the area also did not break 59 percent (New York State Board of Elections 2020). The Hudson Valley is home to competitive state legislative elections.

While these seats are less important in determining the majority due to the overwhelming advantage that the Democratic Party enjoys in the assembly, they are crucial in discerning whether the Democratic Party maintains a supermajority that has the power to overturn gubernatorial vetoes (New York Department of State 2015). Democrats must hold 100 of 150 assembly seats to exercise this power. As of this writing, Democrats have over 100 seats. Thus, the region plays a crucial role in determining this factor.

As such, voters in the area have a part in selecting more than 15 percent of the state assembly and 20 percent of the state senate. More precisely, the region plays a major role in determining the majority of the state senate and whether the Democrats will hold a supermajority in the assembly. Accordingly, it is particularly important to understand the role of progressives in this region due to their potential impact in competitive contests. This is particularly true given the intricacies of New York's electoral system.

More precisely, New York is one of the few states that has a significant third-party presence and allows electoral fusion in general elections. Candidates may run on multiple ballot lines and have their votes on each of those lines fused together. As such, one person may run as the nominee of the Democratic and Working Families Parties. Then, votes the candidate received on each ballot line are added together to produce this person's total vote. That vote is then compared to the vote total for other candidates, who may also appear on multiple party lines.

Yet, third parties are not required to give their lines to major party candidates. This is particularly important when considering whether progressives support the Green Party nominee, a party that is less likely to cross-endorse a Democrat. Further, progressives may choose to vote for a Working Families Party nominee that lost a Democratic primary, thus splitting the center and left-of-center vote. As such, progressives often have another option on the ballot that may harm Democratic Party nominees in a general election.

With this stated, this work endeavors to systematically listen to local progressive politicos to appreciate their involvement in the political arena. It will identify how they are involved in the political world, what tools they use to organize, and how they go about impacting campaigns and public policy. It will also engage the question of whether a progressive identity in the Hudson Valley exists, inquiring to how one's characterization of self stimulates left-wing activism, and whether there are similarities in progressive identities throughout the region. Thus, this project will elaborate on how local progressive activists engage civically and how they consider their own progressive identities in the context of the Hudson Valley.

This study employs a snowball sample. It starts with interviewing well-known progressives in the Hudson Valley and asking those subjects who else should be interviewed. It is not only the county executive and the state senator that interest the author. It is also the local organizer, the volunteer working phone banks, and the mother who joined thousands to head to the Women's March whose voices should be chronicled. This is the story of the people in the trenches of the progressive movement in the region. Their stories should be heard as they can teach us about ideology and activism on the local level of politics and help us to explore if and how that local progressive activism may impact state- and national-level politics.

But why the Hudson Valley and not Brooklyn or Manhattan? The answer is precisely because the Hudson Valley is not part of New York City. It is the opinion of the author that it is commonly believed that progressives can only be found in our nation's biggest cities, like New York, Boston, Seattle, or San Francisco. Yet, this work will illustrate that progressive politicos can also be found in suburban, semirural, and rural areas. This is important because while the work is about the Hudson Valley, it is also about adding to our understanding of how progressives operate outside of America's largest cities. That is the work's second argument. And the book adds to a scant literature highlighting how progressives articulate their ideology outside of America's largest cities.

That is not to say that the Hudson Valley is composed of ten counties of progressives. As my writing on the electorally competitive nature of the area reveals, it certainly is not. It is also worth noting that there are many conservative and neoconservative bastions in the Hudson Valley. In fact, at the 2016 Ulster County Fair, the author observed a high number of individuals sporting Confederate flags on clothing and vehicles. Thus, there are certainly right-wing elements present in the area.

Further, while case studies are common in the analysis of local places, as already stated, the Hudson Valley could be studied more by social scientists. And even though the work will be used to also draw connections to progressives in other places across the nation that are outside of America's largest cities, we still need to understand the Hudson Valley. The region finds itself in an odd place in the New York geographical lexicon, contingent upon where in New York a particular person is born and raised. Thus, it is necessary for readers to become better acquainted with the ten counties explored in this work.

Our Window of Study: Upstate or Downstate?

Map 1.1. The ten counties that compose the Hudson Valley region. *Source:* Created by the author with ArcGIS.

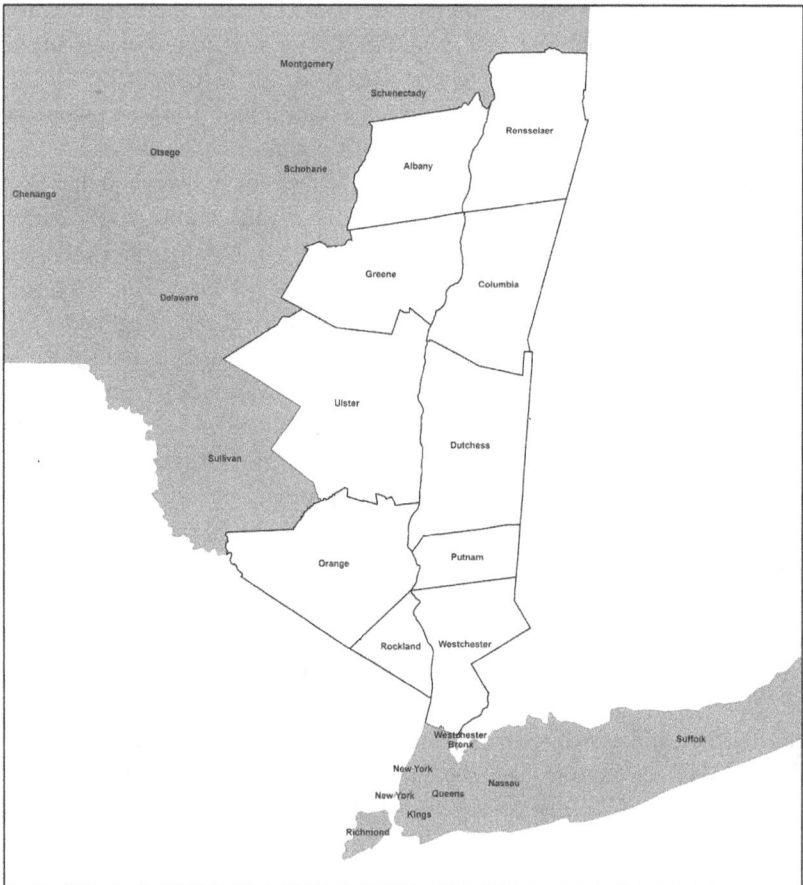

Many individuals born and raised in New York City consider north of the Bronx "upstate." At the same time, many residents of Plattsburgh refer to the Hudson Valley as "downstate." I find it far more useful to ignore such terms. Drawing on the Hudson River Valley Institute, a research center housed at Marist College, the ten counties that comprise the region include: Westchester, Rockland, Putnam, Dutchess, Orange, Ulster, Albany, Columbia, Greene, and Rensselaer Counties (Hudson River Valley Institute).

To help simplify this work, these ten counties, each of which has a border directly on the Hudson River, will be divided into three subregions. The Lower Hudson Valley consists of Putnam, Rockland, and Westchester Counties. The Mid-Hudson Valley includes Dutchess, Orange, and Ulster Counties. The Upper Hudson Valley, also called "The Capital District," comprises Albany, Columbia, Greene, and Rensselaer Counties. To be sure, these counties are diverse. Dividing them into three separate groups helps to organize the region more clearly.

Beyond geography, the US Census Bureau furnishes readers with a wealth of information to help students of the Hudson Valley understand social and economic characteristics of each county studied in this work.

According to the US Census Bureau (2020), each county is majority "white alone," with nine of the ten counties studied being over 62 percent white. In total, 86.1 percent of Columbia County's population identifies with this classification. On the other extreme, Westchester County hosts the smallest number of individuals who identify with this classification, as 52.6 percent of residents fall into this category. It is noteworthy that Westchester is the only county in the study that is below the national average of 60.1 percent of individuals identifying as "white alone."

Westchester and Albany are the only counties examined that are above the national mean for those who identify as black. While the population of the nation is 13.4 percent black, 16.7 percent of Westchester residents and 14.1 percent of Albany residents identify as black Americans. While below the national mean, it is noteworthy that 13.2 percent of Orange County and 13.1 percent of Rockland County residents also identify as black. Nevertheless, black residents in five of the ten counties in this study comprise less than 10 percent of the population.

That said, the percentage of Hispanic residents is more robust. Only Westchester and Orange Counties have populations above the national mean of 18.5 percent, with 25.5 and 21.6 percent of their populations, respectively, falling into this category. Yet, 10.6 percent of Ulster, 12.9 percent of Dutchess, 16.4 percent of Putnam, and 18.4 percent of Rockland identify as "Hispanic or Latino." As such, six of the ten counties have populations

Table 1.1a–d. Data from the 2020 Census for Counties in the Hudson Valley

Table 1.1a. Lower Hudson Valley Census Data

	Percent Bachelor's Degree or Higher	Median Household Income	Median Age	Percent White Alone	Percent Black	Percent Hispanic	Percent of Persons in Poverty	Percent of Government Employees
Putnam County	38.1	$104,486	44.1	77.1	3.9	16.4	5.7	17.9
Rockland County	41.1	$93,024	35.9	62.7	13.1	18.4	14.4	17.2
Westchester County	48.9	$96,610	41.0	52.6	16.7	25.5	7.6	15.0

Table 1.1b. Mid-Hudson Valley Census Data

	Percent Bachelor's Degree or Higher	Median Household Income	Median Age	Percent White Alone	Percent Black	Percent Hispanic	Percent of Persons in Poverty	Percent of Government Employees
Dutchess County	35.0	$81,219	42.8	70.7	12.1	12.9	8.3	15.7
Orange County	30.3	$79,944	36.9	62.7	13.2	21.6	10.6	19.2
Ulster County	32.5	$64,304	44.3	78.8	7.2	10.6	12.7	17.1

Table 1.1c. Upper Hudson Valley Census Data

	Percent Bachelor's Degree or Higher	Median Household Income	Median Age	Percent White Alone	Percent Black	Percent Hispanic	Percent of Persons in Poverty	Percent of Government Employees
Albany County	41.8	$66,252	38.0	71.6	14.1	6.3	11.3	25.1
Columbia County	32.7	$66,787	48.2	86.1	5.3	5.0	10.2	17.7
Greene County	22.1	$53,601	45.9	84.8	6.1	6.3	11.2	20.1
Rensselaer County	32.0	$68,991	39.7	82.6	8.1	5.2	10.4	21.5

Table 1.1d. United States Census Data

	Percent Bachelor's Degree or Higher	Median Household Income	Median Age	Percent White Alone	Percent Black	Percent Hispanic	Percent of Persons in Poverty	Percent of Government Employees
United States	32.1	$62,843	38.5	60.1	13.4	18.5	11.4	14.0

that are over 10 percent Hispanic or Latino, all of which are in the Lower and Mid-Hudson Valley.

Transitioning to other demographic characteristics, seven of the ten counties in this work have populations with an older median age than the nation of 38.5 years (US Census Bureau 2021). Only Rockland, Orange, and Albany Counties, with median ages of 35.9, 36.9, and 38.0, have populations below the national median age. The populations of Columbia and Greene Counties are noteworthy, as the median age of residents of Greene County is 45.9 years and Columbia is 48.2 years. The median age of residents of Westchester, Dutchess, Ulster, and Putnam—while below Columbia and Greene—are also north of 40. Thus, the median age of the populations of most of these counties is also older than the national median age.

Moving to education (US Census Bureau 2020), in comparison to the national mean of 32.1 percent of the population holding a baccalaureate degree, the region is generally highly educated. Almost 49 percent of residents of Westchester hold bachelor's degrees, as do over 41 percent of residents from Rockland and Albany Counties. Further, over 38 percent of Putnam and 35 percent of Dutchess residents hold baccalaureate degrees. Only Greene County, with 22.1 percent of residents holding a four-year degree, is well below the national mean.

Concerning economic characteristics (US Census Bureau 2020), it is noteworthy that the median household income of just one county is below the national median of $62,843. Greene County has a median household income of $53,601. At the other extreme, Putnam's is $104,486 and Westchester and Rockland's are over $93,000. Further, Orange and Dutchess have median household incomes over $79,000 and $80,000, respectively. Thus, median household income is high in comparison to the nation.

Type of employment is linked to income (US Census Bureau 2021). Government is a major employer in the area. The national mean of civilian government employees is 14 percent. The populations of all ten counties in this work are north of that number. On the one hand, only 15 percent of Westchester County inhabitants are government employees. At the other extreme, a full 25.1 percent of Albany County residents are employed by a government, as are over 20 percent of the populace of Greene and Rensselaer Counties.

Additionally, the New York Department of Labor (2016) furnishes us with a useful list of the largest private employers in the region. These include the healthcare industry, research and technology, nonprofit social services, and grocery chains.

Table 1.2. Major Private Employers in the Hudson Valley

Industry	Employer
Health and Hospitals:	Westchester Medical Center
	Crystal Run Healthcare
	Nyack Hospital
	Orange Regional Medical Center
	Albany Medical Center
	St. Peter's Hospital
Research and Technology:	IBM
	Regeneron Pharmaceuticals, Inc.
Nonprofit Social Services:	Center for Disability Services
Grocers:	ShopRite
	Stop and Shop
	Price Chopper
	Hannaford

Hospitals are among the largest private employers in the Hudson Valley, with large numbers of citizens working for Westchester Medical Center, Crystal Run Healthcare, Nyack Hospital, Albany Medical Center, St. Peter's Hospital, and Orange Regional Medical Center. IBM and Regeneron Pharmaceuticals are the most prominent research and technology firms in the area. The Center for Disability Services is also a major employer in the Hudson Valley, as are ShopRite, Stop and Shop, Price Chopper, and Hannaford.

The Hudson Valley also enjoys a robust tourism sector. Many historic sites are found throughout the region. These include the FDR Presidential Library and Museum and the Vanderbilt Mansion National Historic Site in Dutchess; Kykuit, the Rockefeller Estate, in Westchester; the New York State Museum and the Schuyler Mansion in Albany County; and the Martin Van Buren National Historic Site in Columbia. Mohonk Mountain House is located in Ulster County. Beyond these historic sites, there are also seasonal activities.

In the fall, leaf-peeping and pumpkin and apple picking are major attractions, as are apple cider and apple cider donuts. Further, Headless

Horseman of Ulster Park, a venue that provides haunted houses and hayrides, is also a chief attraction. In the winter, skiers descend on Hunter Mountain and Windham Mountain in Greene County, and Belleayre Mountain in Ulster County. There is also a variety of venues to practice snowshoeing. While ice fishing is prominent in the Hudson Valley, the spring begins fishing season, most notably the annual pilgrimage of striped bass. Locals call it "striper season," and the Hudson River is dotted with those hoping to bring home the big one, or at the very least, a legal one. The summer is a time when hikers and campers appear throughout the region, and when the Hudson River is speckled with jet skis, sailboats, and other small watercraft.

Throughout the year, there are fairs and festivals, from flea markets in Stormville, to food and wine festivals such as "Ribfest" in New Paltz, to a hot-air balloon festival in Poughquag. Oktoberfest is also celebrated at different events throughout the region. Simply, locals work hard to highlight the fruits of the Hudson Valley, and there is hardly a time when there is nothing on the calendar. It is a rich region with a proud history that has much to offer residents and tourists alike.

It is also breathtaking, lined with mountains, valleys, quaint towns, bustling arts scenes, and the state's capital. Simply, it is a gorgeous region of our nation if one has the resources to access the bounty of the area.

As stated, it is also home to progressives. It is important to understand what the literature tells us about that term.

Progressive Ideology and American Liberalism

In the United States, the terms *progressive* and *liberal* are often used inter-changeably. Kerbel (2009) articulates that progressives are what "today's liberals prefer to be called" (5). Yet, even if these terms are employed synonymously, each requires qualification and must be understood in the American context (Bell and Stanley 2012).

The term *liberal* has different connotations throughout the world. In the United States, liberals are on the left side of American politics and are typically linked to members of the Democratic Party (Kerbel 2009; Greenberg and Skocpol 1997). To the north in Canada, the Liberal Party is known for its centrist ideology. While in the "land down under," the liberals are found on the right-wing of the Australian political spectrum. Given these stark differences, academics exploring liberal or progressive ideology must be careful to define the term in their scholarship. Indeed,

Gunnell (2001), exploring American liberalism, notes that those using the term *liberal* are required to articulate its meaning clearly; the same is true for those employing the term *progressive*.

The genesis of progressive ideology in America is found in the Progressive Era of the United States (Clucas, Henkels, and Steel 2005; Levine 2000). While some may find it odd to link the activities of today's progressives to the Progressive Era, making this link is important on two fronts. First, progressives in the late 1800s and early 1900s fought for change. In many ways, so do the progressive political activists in this book. Second, and perhaps more importantly, the second chapter of this work will highlight how progressives of today identify with the Progressive Era in the United States. When describing their own progressive ideology, many connect back to the Progressive Era. As such, readers should understand the contours of the term over one hundred years ago so they can understand the term today. Unfortunately, the term was complicated then, as it is now.

During the Progressive Era, the term did not possess a universal definition. Consider the following: "The word progressive, as used around the turn of the century, was so ambiguous as to be virtually indefinable" (Levine 2000, 18). Clucas, Henkels, and Steel highlight that progressives "embraced a variety of different and often conflicting goals" (2005, 2) Yet, all progressives shared a foundation that worked to curb the economic and political influence of America's corporations and asserted that government should advance "the common good" (Clucas, Henkels, and Steel 2005, 2).

Levine too insists that progressives were concerned with a " 'national interest' of 'public good,' superior to special interests and market outcomes" (2000, 18). Further, Levine asserted that progressives resisted libertarian philosophy, as they viewed this ideology as restrictive to the democratic nature of a polity. Thus, while the word *progressive* did not possess a universal definition, progressives largely shared common views on the existence of a public interest and the dangers of corporate influence and libertarian political thought.

Green and Roiphe, reflecting on the Progressive Era, articulate a key point in an explanation of the ideological term. They assert that the movement was by no means "monolithic," but its adherents did indeed worry about societal problems and believed that there should be actions to ameliorate these issues (Green and Roiphe 2020, 723). Thus, for Green and Roiphe, progressives were bound together by a desire to cure the economic and social ills of society that existed in the late nineteenth century.

And then there is Bob La Follette of Wisconsin, widely considered to be one of the founders of the progressive movement in the United States

(Levine 2000). La Follette served as a Republican US representative, governor, and US senator from Wisconsin. He founded the National Republican Progressive League and was the Progressive Party nominee for president in 1924, winning his home state of Wisconsin and carrying almost five million votes nationwide (*Biographical Directory of the United States Congress*; American Presidency Project). Thus, "Fighting Bob" was a national progressive figure.

La Follette insisted, "The will of the people shall be the law of the land" (Levine 2000, xii). Yet, he did not simply believe that the opinion of the majority on a given issue should be converted into policy. Instead, "Fighting Bob" hoped for a polity where citizens were able to participate in political deliberation and, as such, advanced policy goals that worked to include the public widely in political discourse. Accordingly, he yearned for public deliberation and participation unconstrained by corporate, political, or government influences that suppressed the power of the mass public (Levine 2000).

In order to realize this aim, La Follette advanced policy goals that curbed private interests. He conceded that doing so required robust regulatory policy and a well-resourced government bureaucracy to enforce those policies nationwide, since corporations were economic and political actors coast to coast (Levine 2000). Thus, Levine states, "The core of La Follette's Progressivism, in short, was a belief in a fair, deliberative democracy" whose citizenry understood and objectively debated policy nationally without interference from powerful economic or political elites (2000, xiii).

Following La Follette, one must understand FDR and the New Deal, and LBJ and the Great Society, in order to appreciate progressive ideology in the United States (Hart 1997). Hart asserts that two forms of American liberalism emerged out of these administrations.

During the New Deal, the government redistributed economic resources among the citizenry, while during LBJ's time in the White House, the state worked to guarantee rights to women, minorities, LGBTQ+ Americans, and the handicapped (Hart 1997). Thus, progressives in America believe that the state must be employed to promote economic and civil egalitarianism.

In this work, American liberalism (or liberalism) and progressivism will be used interchangeably. While Clucas, Henkels, and Steel (2005) note that progressive may be a crude category, it is the opinion of the author that in today's sense, the two are synonymous as Kerbel (2009) asserts.

With that qualification made, we will look at more literature that endeavors to define American liberalism. Bell and Stanley (2012) equate progressivism, or using their vernacular, American liberalism, with social democracy. It is important to stress that social democracy is not socialism. Social democracy stresses equality, in both social and economic terms (Bell and Stanley 2012). In order to achieve this equality, redistributive economic policies and other legislative initiatives are enforced through government actors. Thus, social democracy, which Bell and Stanley assert is the hallmark of American liberalism, employs the state to usher in economic and social parity.

The state is also central to McCright and Dunlap's work, which endeavors to find an ideological commonality among different progressive social movements (2008). Citing Lakehoff, the authors assert that liberals believe government should be empowered to mitigate both economic and social problems, largely through the use of regulatory efforts and social programs (839). Part and parcel to this, American liberals believe in regulating the economy and also advancing policy that protects those who have been systematically discriminated against (838). As such, the state, and the protection of those who might be exploited, are key in this reading.

Clucas, Henkels, and Steel (2005), too, in their study of ideology in Oregon, focus on the state. These authors assert that progressive activists believe in employing the power of government to fix social problems (2). Thus, again, the power of the state is central to progressive ideology.

DeLeon, in his seminal work on San Francisco (1992), addresses the complexities of defining the term *progressive*, and he, too, asserts that one definition will not work. DeLeon writes, "As used in this book, progressive embraces all meaning of 'Left,' 'Liberal,' and 'progressive.' . . . San Francisco's progressivism is a composite of three distinct Left subcultures and ideological tendencies . . . liberalism, environmentalism, and populism" (32–33). DeLeon notes that liberals generally support government programs that redistribute wealth and an active government that regulates private economic activity in hopes of providing greater equity and social justice. DeLeon articulates that liberals "give highest priority to the goal of equal economic opportunity for poor people and racial minorities, particularly in the areas of jobs, housing, and education" (33). Environmentalists in San Francisco are also heavily interested in active government oversight of the economy. Concerning populism, progressives are locally active and seek to preserve local communities—culturally, socially, and economically—from corporations (33). Thus, for DeLeon, progressives in his work are an amalgam of these three subgroups.

Accordingly, the literature suggests that a key feature of progressive ideology is an active state providing social and economic equity among the populace. As such, government, while not necessarily providing every service and function of society as it would in a fully socialist polity, serves as an arbitrator to ensure that equality and a deliberative democracy are attainable.

But how does ideology correspond to political parties in the United States? McCright and Dunlap are clear to differentiate between ideology and partisanship. While it is true that many liberals or progressives find their home in the Democratic Party, there are many other party organizations with which progressives can affiliate. The Green Party is a national force and the Working Families Party is growing in its influence throughout the nation. There are also Socialist Party branches throughout the United States. While the goals of these three progressive groups are not entirely in unison, those on the left side of the political spectrum fill their ranks. Further, there are a number of state parties throughout the nation that might fill the needs of those on the ideological left, such as the Progressive Party of Vermont, or the Peace and Freedom Party of California. Thus, it is not a necessity that progressives enroll in the Democratic Party.

Yet, given the current partisan composition of our nation's representative institutions, is it realistic for left-wingers, who hope to usher in progressive policies, to not belong to the Democratic Party? Kerbel (2009) and Greenberg and Skocpol (1997) see progressive ideology linked with the Democratic Party. This does not suggest that these authors assert that all Democrats are progressives, but that the party is the main vehicle through which progressives engage in politics.

Kerbel (2009) observes that progressives affiliate with and run for office as Democrats in order to transform the institution into "a genuine progressive party" (3). In this work, Kerbel concedes that the dominant party leadership does not necessarily adhere to a rigid or pure progressive ideology. Perhaps most interesting, Kerbel argues that the purpose of the Democratic Party elite in his study is to simply win elections by forging a coalition of Democratic partisans and independents, while the objective of progressives is to, instead, "create more Democrats" (8). Nevertheless, Kerbel ties the left-wing to the Democratic Party.

Greenberg and Skocpol also connect progressives with the Democratic Party (1997). Yet, their view is somewhat different than other scholars referenced. Instead of simply progressivism that relies on the state to provide equity, these scholars advance what they call a "popular progressive politics" (6).

These authors seek to merge working- and middle-class citizens into an enduring electoral coalition as the Democratic Party achieved during Roosevelt's New Deal. In fact, they warn that Democrats must eschew any indication that they are the party of "cultural liberalism," or care about "the very poor alone," and encompass broader elements in the Democratic Party and in society. Much of this lies in producing an economic policy that meets the needs of diverse parts of the nation and fosters the civic engagement of those in this coalition. Thus, Greenberg and Skocpol's "popular progressive politics" endeavors to achieve a particular type of progressivism within the Democratic Party.

In addition to the party vehicle, to appreciate progressives, students must also understand nongovernmental organizations. Fisher (2006), in her work exploring progressive activism, identifies an array of progressive groups, such as "book clubs; community-supported farms (CSA); cooperatives; environmental groups; lesbian, gay, bisexual and transgender (LGBT) groups; park associations; women's rights groups; and all types of political organizations" (114). Gendron and Domhoff (2009), in their study of Santa Cruz, inform readers that the city's progressive government coalition is composed of "socialist-feminists, social-welfare liberals, neighborhood activists, and environmentalists" (3). Labor, abortion, animal, consumer, and voter rights are also included in the list of causes associated with progressive interest groups (Bell and Stanley 2012; Levine 2000; McCright and Dunlap 2008; Greenberg and Skocpol 1997). Thus, progressive groups are a significant aspect of understanding left-wing activism in the United States.

Accordingly, progressive entities often advocate for the state to employ its resources to achieve economic and social equality among the populace. Concerning New York, left of center activism is present in the literature in a number of ways. One such way is the study of New York's third parties. In particular, Wolfe explored the demise of a prominent left-wing party that existed in the state from the thirties to the fifties—the American Labor Party (1968). The American Labor Party was a prominent third party in New York, whose rise and fall were connected with union support of the organization. Others studied the Liberal Party, in particular, which arose in the forties as an anticommunist third party, fueled by organized labor, who cross-endorsed both Democrats and Republicans in their quest for good government (Armato 2022; Eisner 1969; Soyer 2012, 2022).

Progressive ideology can often be articulated through studying particular communities, municipalities, regions, or states. Thus, we turn to an exploration of the politics of place in a more thorough manner.

The Politics of Place

Case studies maintain a prominent position in the academic literature, particularly in scholarly works that endeavor to understand different states, regions, and municipalities of the United States. While readers will learn about progressives who practice their civic engagement outside of America's largest cities in this work, and draw conclusions about progressive ideology and activism, this scholarship, nevertheless, can be considered a case study of place.

New York City is prominently featured in the academic scholarship of place. In particular, a rich literature exists on the city of New York and the host of political actors that wield power in that metropolis (Kramer and Flanagan 2012; Mollenkopf 1994; Rich 2007; Sanjek 2000). A number of studies also explore particular parts of the Hudson Valley (Duncan and Duncan 2004; Flad and Griffen 2009; Weigold and Yonkers Historical Society 2014). Works exist on studying environmentalism in the Hudson Valley (Lifset 2014; Schuyler 2018). And Kraus (2000) studied Buffalo politics during most of the twentieth century, helping students to understand politics of an upstate city. Other academic works on the state of New York include Kneeland's work on the 1977 blizzard in Buffalo (2021) and Terrie's work on the Adirondacks (1994).

Further, Janette McCoy-McKay interviewed twenty-five party county committee members in a five-county New York Judicial District (2021). Her work explores the perceptions of female county committee members on party recruitment efforts, or lack thereof, of women candidates for public office. The impressive nature of this particular work is the author's interviews with twenty-five local county committee members who have front-row seats in local politics in the state of New York. Thus, New York, one of our nation's largest and most diverse states, has an important place in the academic literature. Yet, more can be done to understand politics in the Hudson Valley.

Accordingly, this work will chronicle power and progressive ideology in the entire Hudson Valley region. It accounts for micropolitical factors outside of New York City but within the political system that governs New York State. It also continues in the tradition of scholarship that studies politics in a particular area through which intellectuals can learn important information to understand particular phenomena more broadly.

Cramer (2016), in her well-regarded book that studies public opinion and rural consciousness in Wisconsin, articulately explains the importance of studying place. She observes, "We should pay attention to place because . . . our system of representation is based on geography, and conflicts between rural and urban areas over who should get what are intensifying . . . But we should also pay attention to place because it is central to the way many people understand the political world" (14).

Indeed, outside of New York City, the state's local government structure is rather complicated. In fact, one could say that local government structures often resemble nesting dolls. One local government often fits into another, and in some cases, even into another municipality.[3] For example, with fewer than ten exceptions, every incorporated village in the state falls within the geographic boundaries of a single town. And every town is within the confines of just one county (US Census Bureau 2012). Thus, a resident of the village of Ravena in southern Albany County casts ballots for a village mayor, a town supervisor, and a county executive. That said, some residents of the Hudson Valley live in cities—and residents of these cities, like Albany, Newburgh, Kingston, White Plains, and Poughkeepsie—vote in citywide and countywide contests. Further, even if every town does not have a village within its borders, every resident of the Hudson Valley has at least two local governments, before even considering school districts and other special districts. As such, scholarship must explain this particular structure more thoroughly.

Thus, my work supports the notion of Clucas, Henkels, and Steel (2005) that "every state has its own political character," and in order to understand that political character, we must explore politics on a microlevel. For example, Cramer (2016), studying rural areas in Wisconsin, observes, "I am arguing that place matters because it functions as a lens through which people interpret politics" (12). Cramer puts her finger on the pulse of "rural consciousness" and how place matters in rural communities. As someone who lived in Wisconsin for four years, this work indeed makes an important contribution not only to the study of Wisconsin but also to the study of politics in areas outside of America's largest cities.

Yet, my project is somewhat different since the progressives that I study in New York reside in urban, suburban, and rural areas. Indeed, progressives in the Hudson Valley can be found in densely and sparsely populated areas of the region. Thus, while Cramer studied rural consciousness and resentment, this work studies progressives in the rural, suburban, and urban regions of the Hudson Valley.

In doing so, I seek to understand if there is a difference among progressives living in the brownstones of Center Square in the city of Albany, in a single-family home on the outskirts of the town of Rhinebeck in Dutchess County, and in an old farmhouse in sparsely populated areas of Woodstock

---

3. School districts, library districts, fire districts, and other special units of local government, most of which have taxing powers, are not included in this formula.

in Ulster County. Perhaps, in these regions, progressivism and the nature of politics is not linked to population density but to other micro- and macropolitical factors? The goal of this book is to explore this question, in addition to understanding the nature of progressives more generally, operating in the context of New York politics, and the micropolitical factors occurring within each county in the region. Thus, instead of rural consciousness in Wisconsin, this book explores the question of whether a progressive identity exists in the Hudson Valley of New York. And, in doing so, it advances an argument that progressives are not only an active and important part of the political theaters in the Hudson Valley but also, more broadly, that they operate outside of America's largest cities.

Thus, this work is about the Hudson Valley. But connections can also be drawn more broadly. In doing so, this work adds to a sparse literature of progressives found in places outside of America's largest cities.

Wayne Fuller (1968), in his work that explores the background of leaders of the progressive movement, observed, "It is true, of course, that not everyone who left the country for the city . . . became a reformer; but it is also true that the majority of those who did become reform leaders came from the farms and small towns in rural America" (2). Reynolds (2000) looks at progressive third-party successes throughout the United States, paying attention to the Vermont Progressive Party's victories, not only with Bernie Sanders but also with state legislators. And Jackson (2021) discusses why the Progressive Party in Vermont has been successful, including the fact that Vermonters are accustomed to small-scale, retail politics where personal connections can be made that bear fruit at the polls. Jackson's work also makes connections with the Working Families Party and fusion voting that takes place both in New York and Vermont. Thus, there is a small literature that takes into account that progressive activists operate outside of America's largest cities. But it is important to note that local structural factors do matter and must be accounted for to understand progressive victories and activities in and out of the Hudson Valley. And, in some cases, like fusion voting in New York and Vermont, there can be similarities that help explain progressive political successes in more than just one region of the United States.

As such, place does indeed matter, as does ideology, more broadly. This work makes contributions to both of these areas. In order to understand the nature of how and why place and ideology matter, this work will engage in a qualitative analysis. Qualitative scholarship is a hallmark of the study of local places. And it often teaches us lessons that can be applied more broadly.

A Qualitative Methodology

Qualitative methodology is about people and places. It is not about people and places buried in large datasets, but people and places as individual entities. The virtue of employing a qualitative lens is that scholars are able to understand the dimensions and contours of our subjects and the geographic regions where they live, work, and practice civic engagement.

Qualitative methodology has a long history in the social sciences. While this work does not study members of Congress or congressional districts per se, any project engaging in qualitative methodology might not be complete without referencing the work of Richard Fenno (1978, 2013).

Fenno followed members of Congress around their districts and, in doing so, not only gained an understanding of their representational personas but the districts that these legislators represented. Fenno presented readers with important descriptions of the populations of each district and the manner in which legislators presented themselves in each part of their constituencies.

In his 2013 homestyle work, Fenno discussed his time with former US Representative Barber Conable of Western New York. While Conable was by no means a progressive, his district, per Fenno, was roughly one-third urban, one-third rural, and one-third suburban. Thus, as we learned a great deal about Conable and his district through a qualitative study, the qualitative nature of the work is important in understanding progressive politicos in New York's Hudson Valley, since this project will be studying urban, rural, and suburban areas.

Cramer (2016) too engaged in a qualitative analysis, but instead of following members of Congress, she spoke to citizens, members of the mass public. The case notes presented in her work discuss in great detail her meetings in rural areas. Through her discussion of focus groups, she paints a clear picture about the utility of qualitative work. Both Fenno and Cramer built relationships with their subjects, told readers about the political worlds they were studying, and made valuable contributions to the academic literature.

In addition to Cramer (2016), a host of other scholars employ qualitative lenses to study local places, such as Cruz (1998), in his study of Hartford; Mollenkopf (1994), in his work on New York City; and Duncan and Duncan (2004), in their book on parts of Westchester County. Indeed, there are too many works to name that have advanced our understanding of local places and the politics of these areas.

All of these projects are not necessarily meant to understand and explain the nature of politics in all places. They seek to study the politics on the microscale, while adding to our understanding of the nature of power more broadly. This book seeks to understand the nature of progressives as they endeavor to gain and exercise power in the Hudson Valley. And, from these lessons, we can think about ideology and civic engagement in other places in the United States.

More precisely, this qualitative work is a constitutive analysis (Cramer 2016; McCann 1996). The endeavor is not to look for causal relationships. It is not even to understand why there are so many progressives in the Hudson Valley. This is an approach that seeks to appreciate the nature of progressives and progressivism. In that sense, it could be considered less of a positivist work and more normative. It is a work that will employ a thick description.

The author endeavors for readers to understand what we can learn about progressives as an entire group and to examine the similarities and differences among progressives in the three different subregions of the area. To do so, the author interviewed progressives involved in political, policy, and civic endeavors. Thus, unlike Fenno, who studied members of Congress, and Cramer, who studied average citizens, my work seeks a middle ground. It studies the people who make politics work: the politically active citizenry who gather petitions, walk door to door, manage Facebook pages, work for progressive causes on the microlevel, organize and attend rallies, and hold nonpaying political party positions. Thus, in order to understand the nature of progressivism broadly, the author spoke to politically engaged progressives in the Hudson Valley and learned about them, their work, their ideology, and their progressive identities.

This project relies on the interviews of sixty-four political activists from the Hudson Valley. Roughly half of the population of the region is found in the counties that compose the Lower Hudson Valley, 30 percent are found in the Mid-Hudson Valley, and the remaining 20 percent in the Upper Hudson Valley. The geographic locations of the sixty-four activists roughly mirror these numbers, and I spoke to subjects from each of the ten counties in the region. Additionally, one of the subjects lives in Schenectady County but is heavily involved with politics in Albany and Rensselaer Counties. As such, this subject provided valuable insights to this project.

I interviewed most of the subjects in one-on-one, semistructured interviews. I spoke to six subjects in groups of two, and three subjects in one group of three. To procure these subjects, I found prominent progressive activists in the region from news stories, social media, and other internet sources. I emailed fifty activists, of which ten replied to my initial correspondence. From there, I employed a snowball sample, asking progressives to refer me to other progressives. Most were Democrats, but a number of Working Families Party and Green Party enrollees contributed to the study. There was even one enrolled Republican in the study. Roughly half of the interviews were in-person and the rest were conducted over the phone or via Skype. These interviews took place between June of 2018 and September of 2019.

Subjects told me how and why they were politically active. They discussed their thoughts on progressive ideology. They explained progressive successes and failures in the Hudson Valley electoral and policymaking arenas, before describing the composition and goals of progressives in the region.

There are several important points that must be communicated concerning the subjects of this study. First, these activists are concerned about the community. No one spoke about their activism being used to protect their own personal fortune or way of life. They each truly and deeply expressed concern about other people, many of whom were less fortunate than themselves. I never left an interview feeling that these individuals are selfish seekers of power to advance their own affluence. Selfless might be a good word to describe these activists. Second, progressives are not just active in their own towns and counties; they are active throughout the region. This is largely due to the way state senate and congressional districts are drawn. They also campaign outside of the Hudson Valley—sending canvassers to Utica, campaigning in presidential contests in Pennsylvania, and making phone calls on behalf of Democratic congressional candidates in other states. Indeed, these activists are busy.

Most interviews lasted around an hour. The shortest was about thirty-seven minutes; the longest was roughly three hours. After these interviews were finished, transcriptions were made and then coded using ATLAS.ti research software. From there, over 350 codes were applied that fall into several major categories, including codes about progressive ideology and the progressive movement, electoral activities, policymaking efforts, and civic engagement that does not fall neatly into electoral or policymaking endeavors. News stories and other documentation supplement the interviews.

A number of activists chose to not reveal their identities in the work. Following the example of Skocpol and Williamson (2016), these subjects were given pseudonyms that appear in italics. Also, the municipalities where these subjects live and work were also given aliases that appear in italics. Furthermore, in an effort to protect identities, and again following the practice of Skocpol and Williamson, certain details that were deemed unimportant were changed.

The work purposely maximizes direct quotations from subjects. Their stories are hallmarks of the electoral, policy, and civic communities in the region. Both to honor their contributions, and for readers to hear what these activists said, the author of this work chose to quote them, liberally.

Concluding Thoughts

The Hudson Valley is beautiful. It stretches from just outside the city of New York, through the Catskills and Taconics, to the foothills of the Adirondacks. It is composed of densely populated urban areas and sparsely settled rural locales that have not been touched by the hands of developers. It has centers of learning, industry, and healthcare. It has a rich and important history, weaved together by the Hudson River. It is also electorally competitive and is home to large numbers of progressives.

To learn about these activists, the author actually spoke to them: the people who make democracy and policymaking work in the region. This book will unpack and support three main arguments: First, that there is a robust and diverse progressive presence in New York's Hudson Valley. Second, that progressive activists are found outside of America's largest cities. And, third, that progressives use the government and nonprofit sector to fight the status quo and advance policies that they believe will usher in equity and equal opportunity.

Thus, we learn about progressive activists in the Hudson Valley, but we also use this study to understand progressive ideology in the United States more broadly. The next chapter provides readers with a dimensional overview of progressive ideology. And it explains the contours of progressive activists more thoroughly. The discourse that follows is an original contribution to the literature in that it continues to shed light on the nebulous term. And it also tells us about these activists. So, let us learn more about these progressives and their ideology.

Chapter 2

The Dimensions of Progressive Ideology and the Contours of Progressives in the Hudson Valley

This chapter has two aims. First, it will illustrate that at the core of progressive ideology is a shared goal toward achieving equity and equal opportunity. Second, it will give readers an overview of the characteristics of progressive activists in the Hudson Valley, and it also begins to unpack the argument that progressives leverage government and nonprofit organizations to fight the status quo as they work to achieve equity and equal opportunity.

Perhaps the most important point of this particular chapter is to highlight the numerous ways that these individuals who make democracy happen think about their ideology. Indeed, progressives themselves are not a monolith, as Green and Roiphe note (2020, 723). Progressives are a quilt of diversity—even if there is an element connecting their ideological predilections.

Before we move on to a dimensional description of the subjects who contributed time to this work, we will first dive into progressive ideology.

Progressivism as an Ideology

THE CONTOURS OF PROGRESSIVE IDEOLOGY

The term *progressive* is, indeed, nebulous. The literature reviewed in this work's first chapter supports the notion that there is not a single definition

(Clucas, Henkels, and Steel 2005; DeLeon 1992; Gendron and Domhoff 2009; Kerbel 2009). And subjects of this work agree. Christine Primomo of Albany observed that there is a great deal of discussion as to what the term actually means. Michael Quackenbush of Dutchess County described the use of the word *progressive* when he proposed the name of the Dutchess County Progressive Action Alliance. When I asked him what progressive means to him, he was not actually sure. He noted that he continued to ask himself this question. As a follow-up, I asked Michael if the word meant anything to him. He responded, "No, that's the thing. It doesn't mean anything. It's a big question mark."

Other subjects agree with Michael Quackenbush. Jen Fuentes, when asked about progressive ideology, also noted that she is no longer sure what the definition means. Rev. Jordan Scruggs told me that she does not like to use the term to describe herself, since she believes it was "co-opted" by regular Democrats as a means of bringing young people who are civically active into the party's fold. She continued, explaining that the term changed over the last ten years. Kat Brezler shared Reverend Scruggs's sentiment, also noting that the term was "co-opted" by those in power. Émilia Decaudin believes that the term has different meanings for different individuals as well, noting that former US Representatives Sean Patrick Maloney and Joe Crowley identifying as progressives is humorous. Decaudin said many people are using the term, and as such, it means almost nothing.

Some think of the word academically—as a place on a political spectrum. Craig Zumsteg defined the term as "anything that is left of . . . the national Democratic line." *Betty Danson* believes "a progressive is to the right of a socialist and to the left of a centrist." *Danson* continued, "I am to the right of socialists and I am to the left of centrists. So that's why I would call myself a progressive." Émilia Decaudin described where she believes progressives fall on a spectrum left of the "center" on a political axis. Decaudin believes that, immediately left of center on the political spectrum, are party regulars in the Democratic Party. To the left of them, you find members of Indivisible, then what Decaudin believes are actual progressives. To the left of real progressives are communists. Others suggested that the term *progressive* simply is the new way for liberals to describe themselves.

John Gromada articulated that conservatives "demonized" the usage of liberal, so progressive replaced the word. He told me, "Liberal was anathema. So, clearly I want . . . progress in the human condition . . . so progressive seems to mean that these days." Julie Goldberg also said that the right made liberal a dirty word, so liberals started identifying by a different label. Goldberg also added a little more to the word to bring it into the twenty-first century. She stated that progressives are liberals "with race and gender consciousness."

Mark Lieberman said plainly that progressive is a synonym for liberal and it was used after Republicans demonized the word. He observed, "So, I think it's just the new liberal, the new Democrat." And Shannon Powell stated that liberal became "tainted" after the demonization by the right, so using progressive is now being "self-aware." Still, the question remains: How does a scholar adequately describe the term *progressive?*

When examining the data collected from sixty-four activists, there is one striking feature that became evident. Progressives believe in fighting the status quo to move the nation toward equity and equal opportunity. And throughout the rest of this work, you will see that progressives believe in the active use of the government and nonprofit sector to achieve equity and equal opportunity. They seek to move the country forward from existing power arrangements that leave out large portions of the nation. Progressives believe it is the duty of either or both the government and nonprofit sector to provide equity and equal opportunity. This could mean protection of the environment, particularly from profitmaking entities. It could mean fighting for social justice—racial, environmental, or economic. It could even mean changing the way campaigns are financed.

These are not individuals who say that the best way for this to happen is by keeping the government out of our lives. Nor are these individuals all socialists who say everything must come from the government. Indeed, many believe in a bottom-up, community-based approach that includes a robust nonprofit sector. Further, they all do not agree on exactly how to go about achieving equity and equal opportunity, nor the degree to which equity and equal opportunity should be pursued. Some progressives would gladly adopt more radical solutions to problems than others. But at the core of their ideology, even if in different degrees, progressives believe in using government and/or the nonprofit sector to move the needle toward equity and equal opportunity. That is the core of progressive ideology.

And progressives speak to this observation. Tom Denton of Ulster County believes being a progressive is found in the struggle between corporations and the people. He believes that the definition of progressive focuses on supporting people before corporations. And he lamented the decline of labor in America. Dr. Barbara Kidney of the Green Party told me that when someone was referred to as liberal, it had a meaning "along the lines of being a Jeffersonian, believing in liberty, and fairness, and nontyranny, and that was fine by me." Ellen Schorsch explained that progressive policy concerns center around those who have been ignored or are not able to advocate on their own behalf. This social justice theme continued.

Columbia County Supervisor Linda Mussmann reported that "fairness, and equal pay, and environment" are key issues for progressives, as well as fighting neoliberalism. Alan Levin asserted that progressives possess compassion and focus on social justice concerns, including helping the impoverished, those without healthcare, people lacking basic necessities of life, and those who do not have "meaningful opportunities to have a meaningful path in life." Levin further articulated that progressives believe that every single person deserves a decent quality of life and that it is not fair for some individuals to profit or gain in a manner that causes others difficulties. Subjects also placed the term in a historical context.

Lucretia George suggested that the term has its genesis in the famous progressive movement of the early 1900s. During that era, labor rights and equality were key issues, as they were during the time of our interview. *George* further argued, "So I would define progressivism as a more liberal way of thinking." *She* stated progressives focus on equality and engaging in actions that benefit the entire population. Included in this view is that progressives believe others are their equals. Dr. Gregory Julian criticized the great wealth disparity in the United States, bemoaning how such a small portion of the population owns such a large part of the nation's wealth. Dr. Julian asserted, "It's just not in keeping with the democratic ethos that I still think is alive . . . 'We the people' means something . . . it's not symbolic. It's not just rhetoric." Dr. Julian told me that being a progressive is a mechanism to create "justice . . . opportunity for us all to make it." Dr. Charles Chesnavage highlighted the needs of the poor and the oppressed.

Dr. Chesnavage explained that progressives endeavor to realize "a more just world and society" by assessing the relationship between currently enacted public policies and how those policies impact the impoverished, underserved, and ignored. Chesnavage articulated that progressives must continue to keep focusing on these individuals or society as a whole will continue to pour resources into jails and homelessness. David Schwartz defined the word as a quest for equality—racial equality, economic equality, and social equality. He noted that these goals define what he works toward. Caroline Fenner affirmed that progressives are not guided by socioeconomic class: "When I'm with people I consider to be progressive, they feel as comfortable on Main Street as they do in Rhinebeck . . . you know, they don't feel that they're too good for certain people."[1] Equity continued to be highlighted by a number of other subjects.

Dustin Reidy explained that progressives work to demolish advantages of one group over another and level "the playing field in both the economy and what we call our social economy." He further articulated that progressives ask if and how a particular policy helps the ignored and the impoverished. John Schwartz told me that "fairness, openness, transparency, equity" describe progressives. Caring about others continued to be highlighted.

Maria Quackenbush declared that being progressive means considering others, so that they have the opportunity to flourish. She noted that this does not focus on cutting taxes, and as such, cutting essential services, simply because a person feels like paying lower taxes. Quackenbush asserted that paying taxes does not bother her since the programs paid for by taxation give everyone an opportunity. Nada Khader observed that progressives insist that everyone should have "basic needs met and guaranteed." Further, people should have access to tools that will help them grow their potential, while not ignoring the earth. Much of this is related to fighting the status quo.

Bart Sooter explained that a chief feature of progressives is their resistance to simply keeping the status quo. *Sooter* noted that they are always looking to make society better. *Sooter* lamented that we, as a society, do not utilize democracy well. Ginny O'Brien, in concert with *Sooter*, also told me that the term is linked to not supporting the "status quo." O'Brien continued, making it known that progressives can find the issues and conditions that need to be changed and then go about doing the work to realize those changes. And Jason Angell argued that progressives endeavor to achieve "deep reform . . . deep institutional systemic change." And, further, fighting the status quo often means fighting for social justice.

Steve Jones explained that progressives advocate for positive changes, generosity, and inclusivity, as well as not ignoring novel ideas and propositions. Caroline Fenner observed that progressivism is about preparing for what comes next. She also argued that the term is about protecting people from unregulated markets and unfettered capitalist greed. Andrew Dalton declared that being progressive is about stopping war and oppression, including oppressive capitalism, "that nobody would do anything for anybody else unless they were paid." Andrew Zink asserted the term connotes fighting the existing status quo to advocate for policies that benefit those who are

---

1. Main Street in Poughkeepsie is an area with high poverty. Rhinebeck is wealthy.

not in the highest classes of society. Connie Hogarth stated that the term is about advocating for new ways of doing things that help everyone. Carolyn Riggs explained the term means not settling for existing structures and arrangements. Again, change is a major theme.

So is inclusivity and equity. Carolyn Riggs told me, "Equality and equity are two very different things. And I believe that everyone should have a fair shot—that there should be nothing that limits an individual from achieving greatness." Christine Primomo articulated that progressive means continuing to move forward and that government policies need to support all people. Primomo also believes that being progressive means continuing to fortify the democratic nature of our polity and paying attention to equity issues that have not been fixed since the nation's founding. Primomo expressed that women, too, should be included in social justice reforms.

Darrett Zephyr Roberts shared similar sentiments and told me that those opposed to progressive ideology want to preserve existing structures that oppose civil rights—including the rights of women. Again, in concert with others, Roberts told me that progressives advocate for policy changes that benefit all. Terence Miller argued that progressives fight existing policy arrangements when they are wrong, particularly when those existing policies are not supportive of the people. So much of the definition, as articulated by the subjects, comes from values.

Jonathan Gross stated that he does not believe in accepting things that are and have been—particularly structural arrangements. He endeavors to move toward what he calls "an ideal." Gross continued, explaining that this ideal comprises inclusivity, collaboration, and advocating for the voiceless and forgotten. This requires bringing people together in economic and socioeconomic terms. Further, he argued that progressives support "personal freedoms."

Reverend Scruggs noted that being progressive is considering the future and "creating spaces of welcome for larger groups of people, expanding our definition of who we consider human." She observed that the nation has incrementally moved toward "recognizing or not recognizing who it is that democracy values. And so, in my mind, being a progressive should mean that we progress in our definition of who and what we value." Marjorie Hsu conveyed similar sentiments, but she also issued a warning about what might happen should society fail to progress toward social justice. Hsu noted that she supports progress, that she hopes to evolve our society correctly. She connected this desire to being a mother, hoping that we, as a society, have compassion and are considerate. Hsu was clear that this progress and the benefits that come from it need to be inclusive of all people, or discord will continue. Pramilla Malick differentiates herself as a "Principled Progressive"; yet this differentiation does not change the main point of moving toward social justice.

Indeed, Malick asserted that there are certain matters where one cannot negotiate. These include health and safety issues, which is how she defines the term *principled progressive*. Malick argued, "We're not going to trade this power plant for that power plant, this pipeline for that pipeline. We're not going to trade the safety of this community for that community." Malick affirmed that these things, related to human rights and life, simply are not going to be compromised. Malick asserts these are standards that cannot be ignored. Somewhat differently, but again in terms of moving forward toward equity, Caroline Fenner believes that progressive ideology is linked to campaign finance.

Fenner observed that progressives are people who endeavor to divorce money from the electoral and policymaking arenas. She told me that this is the nature of being a progressive. Fenner argued that there are individuals who identify as progressives yet do nothing to fix the current structure of campaign finance. As such, she believes that they are not actual progressives because they benefit from existing arrangements. Obviously, everyone does not benefit from the current campaign finance system. Again, moving forward toward equity: That is the hallmark of how progressives articulate their ideology. And, in Fenner's case, that is linked to reforming campaign finance.

Again, this section illustrates that the main goal of progressive ideology is moving forward toward providing equity and equal opportunity. This does not mean that every progressive believes in the same means for achieving equity and equal opportunity. And it does not mean that every subject believes that the government or the nonprofit sector should provide perfect equality. But it is truthful to say that each of the subjects who contributed time to this work believe in fighting the status quo to work toward providing more equity and equal opportunity throughout the nation than exists at the present.

Progressives

Understanding motivations of those who are civically engaged is an important part of any political study. Clark and Wilson (1961) discuss different incentives that are realized in distinct types of organizations. They write that activists may possess motivations that include material, solidary, or purposive benefits (129). They observe that material incentives are linked to some "tangible 'fringe' benefits," often related to financial capital of some sort (134). Solidary incentives are similar to social capital (Putnam 2000)—norms of reciprocity and trust that develop from interpersonal interactions—along with a sense of kinship, identity, and even "fun" that comes from engagement in an organization or movement (Clark and Wilson 1961, 135). Finally, Clark and Wilson highlight purposive incentives—the accomplishments that an organization endeavors to achieve. These motivations are important to understand, as is a typology of civically engaged individuals that Roscoe and Jenkins (2016) assert falls into two main categories.

Roscoe and Jenkins (2016) discuss the differentiation between party organizers and party activists in their book studying local party organizations. The authors claim that party activists, who, despite receiving a benefit outlined by Clark and Wilson (2016), "must be viewed more as resources than as actors who direct those resources" (14). These individuals are on the front lines of the political arena—acting as the arms, feet, and voices of political parties. They implement the strategy and policies that are determined by party organizers, who are constantly engaged in planning and establishing an infrastructure for party activities to be carried out. For organizers, there is no off-season in the political game. They routinely hold party office. That said, Roscoe and Jenkins acknowledge that there is often a route from party activist to party organizer. For the purposes of my work, the term *political activist* is used to encompass the spectrum of those who are civically engaged in power politics—whether they are an activist, an organizer, or somewhere in between—as defined by Roscoe and Jenkins.

These progressive political activists are found throughout the Hudson Valley. This project took me throughout the region. I traveled to the majestic peaks of Bear Mountain in Rockland County's town of Stony Point, to the mighty mountaintop of the village of Tannersville in Greene, to a tiny organic farm nestled in the serene Taconic Mountain Range of Putnam County. I visited the cities of Albany, Kingston, Yonkers, Hudson, White Plains, and Poughkeepsie. I was in the towns of Irvington, Yorktown, Bethlehem, Hyde Park, Nyack, New Paltz, and Esopus. I spoke to subjects from East Greenbush, Windham, Beacon, Tuxedo, and Spring Valley.

Progressive activists come to us from every demographic—Asian, white, black, and Hispanic. They are wealthy and live paycheck to paycheck. They are young and aged, with some subjects in their early twenties and others over eighty and ninety. They are college students and youth coaches, teachers and professors, organic farmers and nonprofit executives, librarians and stay-at-home dads, engineers and economists, campaign managers and nurses. They are elected officials, party officials, appointed officials, and hold no government or party offices at all.

And, indeed, many activists and organizers operate inside party structures, outside party structures, and in both theaters. They are as demographically diverse as America.

DIVERSITY OF LENSES

I asked subjects to describe their fellow progressives. Three takeaways came from these interviews. First, progressives are diverse. Second, there is a variety of lenses through which they see their fellow progressives. Third, they approached this question rather differently.

One subject used the word *oppressed* as a lens to describe progressives. *Lucretia George* observed that progressives cannot be typecast by demographic labels. Indeed, she said progressives are diverse. She noted that progressives often include people of color and also those from religious groups that have many people of color as adherents. *George* declared that progressives are those who often find themselves oppressed or are trying to ameliorate the conditions of the oppressed. Others highlighted occupations.

Marjorie Hsu of Westchester told me about the diversity of her group of progressive activists. She told me that her group contains people in the arts—graphic artists and photographers. There are also people who work in the technology sector, academics, and parents who stay at home to take care of children. Hsu explained that the group's diversity is its strength, and that these different people, with different backgrounds, have been able to collaborate effectively. Subjects also provided a typology of progressive activists in the area.

John Schwartz observed that there is a "strong, labor-working class, Democratic demographic contingent." Further, he articulated that a core of active progressives are former residents of the city of New York. He noted that many of these former New York City residents might have owned second homes in the region, previously, and then decided to move to the Hudson Valley permanently, enriching the area with their urban policy perspectives. And he was not the only person to discuss the impact of those who moved into the area from the five boroughs. Pat Strong attested to the large number of residents moving into the Hudson Valley from New York City, fortifying the progressive presence in the region.

Beyond the dimensions already noted, many subjects described progressive activists by their age and generation.

GENERATIONS

The differences in the age of progressive activists are important to chronicle. One subject who was well under forty asserts that the progressive movement is a place for young people. Many subjects believe that the progressive movement is largely older, while others say it is multigenerational. Indeed, there is a diversity of perspectives on this matter.

Many progressives in Greene County appear to be older than sixty. Ellen Schorsch of Greene County observed that her group is thrilled when they have new members who are younger than sixty. Dr. Ron Lipton, also of Greene County, lamented that there are not more younger activists as involved in progressive activism "as they should be." This observation is not unique to Greene County.

Per Julie Goldberg of Rockland, older women compose one of the pillars of the progressive foundation in her county. Goldberg observed, "They fear neither God, nor man." One of these women knocked on a person's door whose home displayed a lawn sign for Goldberg's primary election opponent, State Senator David Carlucci. Goldberg recounted that this older activist told the homeowner that she was there to talk about Senator David Carlucci and explain why the homeowner should not display Carlucci's sign. Julie noted, "Older women know where the bodies are buried" going back thirty years. She also asserted that older women raise money and have very long memories. That said, Goldberg also observed that progressive organizations in Rockland County need younger people.

In addition to labor, and expatriates from New York City, John Schwartz made known that progressives have been a prominent feature of the region since the hippies during the 1960s. These former hippies still articulate their progressive ideology today. He noted that one of the main reasons for this group's activism is found in opposition to the Vietnam War, and that life experience still fashions their thoughts and actions. John Gromada supported this observation, explaining that many activists north of sixty were involved in "ex-hippie culture."

Jen Fuentes described the age of attendees at Faso Fridays. Faso Fridays were gatherings every Friday in front of one of former Rep. John Faso's district offices to protest his stances on a variety of issues. And several activists told me how colorful these actions were, even featuring a progressive marching band at one gathering. Fuentes noted that most Faso

Friday protesters were over sixty, not younger activists. Fuentes explained, "Some of these folks are . . . dusting off their lefty, after taking a bit of a slumber . . . I've had some interesting conversations with some of the folks about like, the antiwar things that they were involved in." As such, Jen Fuentes too articulates a sentiment shared among a number of subjects that many progressives are older.

Other subjects reported that there are progressives younger than sixty. Dolores Baldasare observed that she met many progressive activists who range from forty to seventy years in age. Susan Van Dolsen of Westchester noted that there are activists in her group that are younger and older than her. But she lamented that there were not many activists younger than forty. And other subjects say that the movement is truly multigenerational.

Lucretia George told me she knows progressives of all ages. *Thelma Davidson* agreed, noting that progressive activism in *Saint Ives* is multigenerational, with activists in their twenties and thirties who come to *Saint Ives* from across the nation. *Davidson* affirmed, "This whole infusion of new people into activism in the Democratic Party, outside the Democratic Party . . . is really a healthy sign of democracy." And others note the prominence of young people.

Andrew Zink insisted that the progressive movement is for younger people, noting that, at the time of our interview, several officers of the Ulster County Democratic Committee were younger than thirty-two years of age. Zink continued, noting that at least two Democratic nominees for Ulster County Legislature were under thirty-five, and that Pat Ryan became Ulster County Executive when he was thirty-seven years old. Further, Zink noted that there are large numbers of younger activists that are influential voices in the progressive movement. That said, like *Thelma Davidson*, Zink observed that the movement contains more than just younger activists. He told me, "It is older people. It is men. It's women; it is everyone. The progressive movement is growing and expanding and it's happening across all demographics, but it is certainly being led and energized by young people."

From these statements, it can be extrapolated that there are progressive activists of all ages. Beyond age and generation, there was a great deal of discussion among subjects about the racial and gender balance of progressives.

Race and Gender

Several subjects provided important information on racial and gender components of progressive activists. Tasha Young addressed racial differences among progressives.

Young observed that progressives in the region often fail to fight inequality in the manner that many people of color would find appropriate. She told me that many progressives focus on environmental and healthcare concerns, and do not address economic inequality forcefully. She noted that in her county, progressive activists would support things if they do not impact their own livelihoods or raise their own taxes. Young argued that this is different from many people of color who often must fight for their lives simply because of the color of their skin. Young continued reporting, "If you have at times, the progressives, who are not people of color, getting involved with you know, letting people know about ICE raids. You know, doing race equity to the extent that they know what that is, but still supporting candidates that are not on board with that . . . as a person of color, I'm like, how is this progress?" Thus, Tasha Young explained a great deal about how activists of color view activism and ideology.

Several progressives highlighted their efforts to integrate their groups. John Gromada told me of his goal of bringing people of color into the progressive movement and noted the challenges and constant work to try to do so. Shannon Powell explained the racial makeup of Indivisible groups. Powell noted that many activists in Indivisible Westchester are largely women, but they are working to build diversity. Powell continued, noting that one of her organization's African American members is working to empower other people of color through monthly phone calls hosted for Indivisible members who are of color. Powell reported that Indivisible Westchester is attempting to diversify, also telling me that there is an Indivisible Latino group. And she noted that since there are so many Indivisible groups scattered throughout the county, some groups are more diverse than others, noting the diversity of the New Rochelle chapter, in particular.

Subjects indicated that many progressives, but not all, are white. And Young revealed how black activists think differently than white activists about issues. Further, white activists are working to diversify the movement. Thus, this section sheds light on information about the composition of the progressive movement and how activists seek to diversify.

The November 2016 General Election

All subjects in this study can be broken down into one of two classifications. First, a large number of subjects have been actively engaged in the electoral, policy, and civic arenas for years. Second, roughly an equal number of activists became heavily involved only after the election of Donald Trump in 2016. These newer activists were horrified by the election and chose to work to oppose President Trump and the Republican Party.

Carolyn M. Riggs of Greene County recalled that she did not remember a progressive movement in the area prior to the 2016 election. She noted that progressive activists joined so many others throughout the country in becoming civically engaged after President Trump won in 2016. Case in point is Ellen Schorsch of Greene County. Schorsch told me that she became active following the 2016 General Election, founding a group in Windham, which she described as a small group of women who "just got together and screamed, and yelled, and cried." Jonathan Gross, also of Greene County, who belongs to Mountain Top Progressives with Schorsch, noted that four women got together to lament the results of the election and then invited others to join. Gross said, "It started as therapy and ended up as political action."

Many other progressives share similar stories. Carolyn Guyer stated that she became active in 2017, due to the results of the 2016 contest. Craig Zumsteg told me the same. He became involved after President Trump won in 2016. He noted that he was not unaware of political news, but he never thought it was his job to participate until that point. Other activists became reengaged.

Dr. Gregory Julian was politically active for decades prior to the 2016 election but took a hiatus in his activity in the years leading up to it. When Trump won, he told his wife that he was becoming politically active once more, starting with local organizing. Many other activists who have been involved for decades tell of the massive number of new activists that became engaged as a result of the 2016 General Election.

Lin Sakai of Ulster County explained, "Let me just step back to last year . . . the whole Trump election and the resistance. Because a lot of people came out of it . . . You wonder where have you been all my life?" Émilia Decaudin of Westchester reported that many activists in Indivisible became active after the 2016 General Election, and many activists for Bernie Sanders were very involved in 2015 or early 2016, organizing and volunteering for Sanders. Maria Quackenbush of the Dutchess County Progressive Action Alliance recalled that over sixty-five people attended her group's meeting after President Trump won. And Christine Primomo of Albany told me about CapitalWomen, started in December of 2016 by women who were distressed about the election. Since then, Primomo noted that the group ballooned to over six hundred members. Other activists throughout the Hudson Valley explained the surge in activism.

Connie Hogarth observed that the progressive movement expanded due to Trump's election win. Hogarth continued, describing a sprouting of a large number of progressive organizations in the area, similar to but not only including Indivisible. Connie also told me of discussions with other activists who hoped to dialog and find commonalities among these different groups. She asserted, "It's like a bunch of seeds that have been strewn and are taking hold and influencing both political choices and also the undercurrent of activism . . . People are just organizing." Jason Angell of Putnam County also confirms this upswell of activism following November of 2016.

Angell made known too that there has been a proliferation of progressive groups, including Indivisible, and also "resist Trump groups." He estimated that roughly half of those organizations were still functioning at the time of our interview. Angell continued, explaining that a large portion of the existing efforts have run their course and are no longer as active as they were, but, he believes this engagement had an enduring impact. He observed that a number of people reacting initially to the election have gone back to their previous lives, but many groups are still active and functioning. Again, November 2016 was a major focusing point for progressive activists.

Angell also revealed that progressive activists realize the disjointed nature of all these groups, but at the time of our interview, activists began the process of connecting them, either into one broad organization, or at least, coordinating them to work around an issue or effort in several of the region's congressional districts. Angell told me that it is unquestionable that the election brought forward a great deal of progressive activism. As such, a large number of individual activists who gave their time to this study did not begin to articulate their activism until after the 2016 General Election.

The next section highlights a number of groups that progressives use to articulate their activism. Subjects told me about many of these groups. They are legion.

PROGRESSIVE GROUPS

A large number of subjects chronicled the activities of progressive groups in which they are active or that operate in their counties. Most of the groups that progressives told me about are not single-issue organizations but involved in a constellation of progressive issues and causes. Dr. Barbara Kidney, a Green Party cochair in the region, described the scene: "Well, to me, it's like a hodgepodge of different groups and just arranged around different issues, and different people . . . basically ill-organized, but sometimes it works." Pat

Strong chronicled the large number of progressive groups in the area. Strong asserted that there was a great change in the number of activist organizations since she became active in the region well before the 2016 election. Strong was heartened by this, as she noted that prior to this upswell of groups, progressive activism was largely centered in the Democratic and Working Families Parties. Strong affirmed that these groups contributed a great deal of discourse and engagement to progressive activism in the region: "And so, kind of like, let a thousand flowers bloom here." Groups exist throughout the Hudson Valley.

Members of Indivisible contributed a great deal of their time to explaining the activities of progressives in their individual counties throughout the Hudson Valley. There are Indivisible groups in each and every county in the Hudson Valley (Indivisible n.d.a). Indivisible was founded immediately after Donald Trump's victory in order to organize at the local level, "to pressure your elected officials to resist Trump's agenda" (Indivisible n.d.b). The genesis of this organization is found in a widely circulated Google document—a guide to tell progressives how to organize. Groups started forming throughout the country, using this document as a blueprint. Indivisible formed in opposition to President Trump and is now well established nationally. Other groups in this study have been around far longer, such as Westchester People's Action Coalition (WESPAC).

Nada Khader is the current executive director of WESPAC, a nonprofit founded by another subject who gave time to this study, Connie Hogarth. Khader explained that her organization was very active in the effort to ban fracking in New York and also to advocate for bail and discovery law reforms, as well as banning solitary confinement in the state. Its website declares, "WESPAC Foundation has been a leading force for progressive social change in Westchester County, New York, since 1974. We have been educating, agitating and organizing for a more just and peaceful world, an end to militarism and racism and a more fair economy that works for all" (Khader 2013).

Dolores Baldasare explained that when she thinks about progressives, Rockland United comes to her mind. Rockland United's website says the following: "We are and stand with people of color, LGBTQIA, women, men, immigrants and survivors. We are anti-racist, pro-patriotic, pro-immigrant, inclusive and peaceful" (Rockland United n.d.). The website also tells readers that the group is committed to progress and protecting civil rights for the most vulnerable. And the website offers a description of how they go about doing so, which includes hosting community events to educate local residents, building social capital and networking, and raising money for groups and candidates. There are other groups in Rockland.

Jacquelyn Drechsler mentioned the Rockland Coalition to End the New Jim Crow, which she praised for their recent work. Its Facebook page declares that this group endeavors to stop government from using "the criminal justice system as a tool of racial oppression" (Rockland Coalition to End the New Jim Crow n.d.). This includes work locally, in Rockland County, and more broadly. The social media page also noted they seek structural and societal changes as they endeavor to achieve "racial equality in America." Drechsler also told me about the Rockland Citizens Action Network.

According to their website, the Rockland Citizens Action Network has many members who became politically engaged during the 2016 presidential campaign of Bernie Sanders. They also report that they endeavor to network with others who hold the same values they do, in order to construct a "mutual support system that progressives will need if [they're] going to be successful." Indeed, a large number of subjects that gave their time to make this study possible were active in Rockland Citizens Action Network.

Émilia Decaudin told me names of other progressive groups in the area, such as the Lower Hudson Valley Progressive Action Network that came out of the Sanders 2016 campaign. Decaudin also mentioned statewide progressive groups—including Citizen Action of New York, Make the Road New York, and New York Communities for Change—who are the core of the Working Families Party. Per Decaudin, the Working Families Party and these three groups share leadership. The Mid-Hudson Valley also has progressive organizations.

The Dutchess County Progressive Action Alliance is a well-known group that will be discussed prominently in the upcoming chapters. Their website states that they marshal political engagement from Dutchess County residents to achieve progressive policy goals (Dutchess County Progressive Action Alliance 2021). As will be discussed, they break their organization into action teams that mobilize around certain issues such as healthcare and social justice.

In the Capital District, Christine Primomo mentioned Swing Left and the local chapter of the American Civil Liberties Union (ACLU). Swing Left states their mission is to build an enduring ethos of local political engagement that results in electoral victories (Swing Left n.d.). Similar to Indivisible, the group was created after the 2016 General Election. Per Swing Left's website, the group has two affiliates in the Hudson Valley—one in Ulster

County and another that happens to also be an Indivisible group (Swing Left n.d.a). Thus, progressive groups from different organizations affiliate with each other and share information.

Another group with a prominent presence, and whose stories will appear in the following pages, is Mountain Top Progressives in Greene County. Their website affirms their commitment to improving the community and the nation by advocating for "universal values of peace, economic prosperity, environmental integrity, social equality and justice for all." Jonathan Gross of Mountain Top Progressives reported that the group is creating "a template" for activists to become engaged. The case of Mountain Top Progressives, in particular, illustrates that even in reliably Republican counties of the region, progressive groups exist and are a noticeable part of the political landscape.

Maria Quackenbush observed that progressive groups were "popping up like popcorn all over the place there for a while." Given the proliferation of Indivisible and Swing Left groups after the 2016 General Election, that observation is extremely appropriate. To understand progressives, it is important to first appreciate the large number of groups that exist throughout the region through which they articulate their activism. The proceeding chapters will highlight the differences between their approaches. Some, like Swing Left and NY19 Votes, focus on elections. Others, such as WESPAC and the Dutchess County Progressive Action Alliance, focus on issues. And a number, such as Mountain Top Progressives and Indivisible, navigate between elections and policy. Nevertheless, group activism is a major part of progressive civic engagement in the region, and these groups, and many others, will be highlighted in the following chapters.

Progressive Diversity

This section is meant to illustrate the diversity of progressive activists in the Hudson Valley. Different professions and outlooks of progressives are highlighted, as are generational differences. Progressive activists are all ages—as evidenced not only by the data presented here but by the sample interviewed for this project. Vicenarians, tricenarians, octogenarians, and even a nonagenarian all contributed to this study. Further, the work chronicles an important point: many of the activists in this study were not politically engaged until November of 2016. And many of the groups that these activists articulate their civic engagement through did not exist prior to November of 2016. Indeed, the election of Donald Trump was the catalyst that infused a new group of activists into the Hudson Valley to add to the already engaged base of progressives who have been articulating their ideology in the region for decades.

Importantly, in line with a major argument of this work, progressive involvement in these groups illustrate that they are a robust presence in the Hudson Valley. Further, the proliferation of these groups throughout the region illustrates clearly that progressives are not only denizens of America's largest cities. Indeed, progressive activism is much more pervasive, even found in rural areas like Greene County. And these groups are nonprofit vehicles through which progressive activists fight the status quo in support of equity and equal opportunity by seeking to win elections and/or adopt desired policy changes.

Conclusion

The purpose of this chapter was twofold. First, it articulated the main points of progressive ideology as described by left-wing activists themselves. And second, it gave readers an overview of left-wing activists in New York's Hudson Valley and outside of America's largest cities. Progressives work to defeat the status quo in their attempt to move toward equity and equal opportunity.

The next three chapters highlight two things. First, they underscore the robust and visible progressive presence in the region. And second, they chronicle the means of how progressives will use the government and nonprofit sectors to fight the status quo and advance their march toward equity and equal opportunity. Chapter 3 focuses on parties and elections. Certainly, participating in the party structure and capturing government is a way to advance toward equity and equal opportunity.

Chapter 3

Progressive Activists in the Electoral Arena

There is a robust progressive presence in the Hudson Valley and these progressive political activists use the government and nonprofit sectors to fight the status quo in order to march toward equity and equal opportunity. This chapter illustrates the integral role progressives play in making democracy function in the region. They engage and educate voters and are an important part of ensuring campaigns exist and operate. And many hold key positions in three different political parties. In order to achieve their goals, progressives seek to nominate and elect officeholders who share their values.

Political Party Involvement

Many progressives are heavily engaged in the political party structure of the Democratic, Working Families, and Green Parties. In their roles, they run for county and state committee seats. Many also run for delegate to their national conventions. They leverage their positions, sometimes to breathe new life into a party, either by taking over seats that are open or vacant, or running primary challenges against longtime committee members. They also ensure that parties are in positions to nominate candidates for public office or other party positions. Indeed, political parties are important actors in the campaign process. And, due to New York's system of fusion voting that allows candidates for public office to run on multiple ballot lines and have their vote totals combined, third parties also matter. As such, progressives are an important component in the party structure and use their committee seats to impact party nominations for public office.

In New York, each major party elects at least two county committee members from each election district, the smallest political unit in the state (New York State Board of Elections 2021). An election district is "the basic political subdivision for purposes of registration and voting" (New York State Board of Elections 2021). In other states, it is often referred to as a precinct. Importantly, in counties outside of the city of New York, an elected county committee member can have numerous roles.

Elected county committee members who do not reside in New York City also sit as members of their party village, town, or city committees by virtue of their county committee position (New York State Board of Elections 2021a). In New York, with rare exception, all villages are found within the geographical boundaries of a single town. And all towns are within the geographical boundaries of a single county. Each village has at least one election district that elects two county committee members for a given major party.

As such, should a county committee member hold a county committee seat representing an election district in a village, that county committee member is also a member of their village committee and their town committee. Thus, county committee members outside of New York City often have at least two roles to play. In the case of a county committee member representing an election district in a village, they have three roles to play—finding candidates to run for village office, in addition to town and county offices.

Progressive activists in the Hudson Valley are actively engaged as village, town, and county committee members. Mark Lieberman, a member of the Yorktown Democratic Committee in Westchester, ran for the post in order to affect the party beyond being a volunteer and worked to encourage others to fill open committee seats. Lieberman expressed, "And that helps us go from a fairly lethargic Democratic committee to a more visible, more active Democratic committee." John Gromada, a party volunteer and member of the Democratic committee from Rockland County, expressed that he has been endeavoring to bring "local progressives, left-wing people," into his county committee in order to change the county party. And Dr. Maria May recounted that the Tuxedo Democratic Committee was inactive until a town supervisor candidate restarted the committee. Dr. May recalled that the candidate stimulated participation by sending mail to all Democrats in Tuxedo. Due to his efforts, the committee now has monthly meetings with over twenty-five attendees. As such, progressive activists work to breathe new life into committees.

Progressives also served as committee officers. Andrew Zink was the treasurer of the Ulster County Democratic Committee at the time of our interview. In this position, besides managing the financial aspect of the party, he also works with local town committees in the county to increase their social media presence, manage their own finances, and improve their outreach to voters. And Kat Brezler of Westchester noted that she is a district leader who also held the position of recording secretary for the City of White Plains Democratic Committee.

In some instances, progressives fought for their committee seats in primary elections and also organized contests for numerous committee seats. Steven White was part of Ramapo Democrats for Change. In 2008, this group launched an organized county committee primary campaign against sitting committee members of Ramapo. Per White, his group won a majority of seats in that primary election, even defeating incumbent party officers. He also lamented that the opposing slate used legal maneuvering to stay in power after scheduling three conventions to elect officers through a process of declaring proxy votes that Ramapo Democrats for Change held as invalid.

Supervisor Linda Mussmann of Columbia County told me about her time as the head of the City of Hudson Democratic Committee and her successful campaign to win county committee seats in the city of Hudson. She recounted, "So it was really cool that we took it over and that . . . came about because we had a tremendous fight here in Hudson over the St. Lawrence Cement Plant." Additionally, subjects also chair different committees.

Dr. Gregory Julian became chair of the Town of Stony Point Democratic Committee after the 2016 General Election. He recalled that one of his first actions was to draft a resolution asserting that the Rockland County Democratic Committee would not support any member of the Independent Democratic Conference[1] in the New York State Senate. He noted that this was "radical" but delighted in telling me that the motion passed by a margin of 150 votes. He noted that the committee members who voted for the resolution, many of whom were mainstream to moderate

---

1. The Independent Democratic Conference (IDC) was a small group of New York state senators elected as Democrats who did not join the larger Democratic conference in the chamber. The IDC joined forces with senate Republicans and, in a power-sharing agreement, provided the votes needed to keep the Republicans in the majority, even though more Democrats were elected to the senate.

Democrats with a long tenure on the committee, were extremely bothered by the Independent Democratic Conference.

Carolyn M. Riggs from Greene County was the chair of the Town of Hunter Democratic Committee and, additionally, the Greene County Democratic Committee at the time of our interview. Beyond recruiting and campaigning for candidates for public office, much of Riggs's job is ensuring compliance with party bylaws, state election law, and campaign finance policy. She described these administrative tasks, including running and organizing nominating caucuses, filing paperwork, and recruiting Democrats to serve as election inspectors in every election district. Additionally, a great deal of time was spent on fundraising and designating petitions for those running for party positions and public offices.

Beyond holding positions at the local level, progressives are active at the state level. Both Carolyn Riggs of Greene County and Émilia Decaudin of Westchester, the latter of whom was running for Democratic state committee at the time of our interview, explained that Democrats elect state committee members from portions of assembly districts within a county. Beyond running for state committee in Westchester, Émilia noted that due to heavy voter turnout in Westchester County, state committee members from Westchester have some of the most powerful seats on the Democratic state committee. State committee members each have a weighted vote based on voter turnout in the unit they are elected from, which puts many of these Hudson Valley political activists in powerful positions.

Beyond running for state committee in Westchester, Decaudin also recruited people to run for state committee positions in other parts of the state. Émilia reported that she helped individuals in Tioga County and another in Tompkins County in their quests for state committee posts, in addition to candidates in Syracuse and potentially Rochester. Émilia worked on ballot access for most of these candidates. Most of these state committee candidates ran as Sanders delegates to the national convention. Decaudin told me that running for state committee and encouraging others to do so was about showing a progressive presence on the state committee. Indeed, Decaudin's participation and the activism of many other progressives stemmed from Bernie Sanders and his 2016 campaign for the White House.

Decaudin observed, "Bernie got like 40 percent of the vote here. Maybe we're not the majority . . . but we're not like three people. So, the idea is to increase our representation to the committee or in the county committees." Decaudin continued that it was not possible for their campaigns to overtake the whole of the state Democratic committee. Instead, Decaudin's goal was to show the state committee that progressives have a strong presence in the room, not simply a few stray voices. Decaudin explained that the way to change the party is to fill party positions with like-minded individuals—not to suggest that their job is to fight existing committee members, but simply to be represented in the party organization. Thus, party position holders like Decaudin have an impact on local committees and also on the state committee.

The impact of the Sanders campaign could also be seen in progressive activists running and winning delegate positions to the national convention. Kat Brezler recounted her experience running for the position while supporting Bernie Sanders in 2016. She told me that she was among the first organizers for Sanders and organized the nominating petitions to place Sanders and his slate of delegates and alternate delegates on the primary ballot. Brezler recounted that she ran as a Sanders delegate in 2016 and won the highest number of votes in the presidential primary out of all delegate candidates committed to Sanders in the seventeenth congressional district of New York.

The evidence clearly illustrates that progressive activists in the Hudson Valley are engaged in microlevel politics in their towns, cities, and counties. They run for state committee and help others to run for committee seats. Furthermore, they seek positions as national convention delegates. Indeed, progressives are heavily involved in Democratic Party politics. But that is not the entire story of progressive involvement in political parties.

WORKING FAMILIES PARTY ACTIVISM

Craig Zumsteg is a Working Families Party activist and gives input on granting the Working Families Party line to nonparty members in general elections due to New York's system of electoral fusion. Fusion permits candidates to run on multiple ballot lines and have the vote totals received on each line combined for the purposes of determining a winner (Benjamin 1974, 44). A large part of this process is assessing candidate questionnaires. Craig Zumsteg explained that those seeking the party nomination complete a questionnaire that is over thirty pages and are then interviewed by the endorsement com- mittee. After that, committee members vote and the scores are referred to state Working Families Party officials. It is clear that the Working Families Party is interested in the positions of candidates who appear on its ballot line, and progressive activists spend a great deal of time helping the party determine whom to give its nomination to for public office.

Steve Redler, a Working Families Party state committee member, told me he actively campaigns for candidates and works to have voters cast their

ballots on the Working Families Party line. Redler told me of the importance of the Working Families Party in general elections, leveraging the
power of fusion rules. He asserted that many citizens who cast ballots on
the Working Families Party line might have voted on the Democratic line,
but not all of them would have done so. He recounted the story of former
Bethlehem town supervisor John Clarkson winning his post by a mere ten
votes. Redler expressed that Clarkson received four hundred votes on the
Working Families ballot line and noted that he believed this ballot line
delivered the election to Clarkson. He proclaimed that it is highly unlikely
that 390 voters would have all voted for Clarkson on the Democratic line.

Beyond the importance of the Working Families Party in the electoral
coalitions of candidates for public office, Steve Redler professed that he is
an informal party organizer for the WFP in the town of Bethlehem. In this
organizing role, he sends mailings to every party registrant in his town and
visits each of these party enrollees during petition time because he endeavors
to meet every WFP enrollee. He noted that many other individuals who
gather petitions for Working Families Party nominees obtain enough signatures to qualify candidates for office, with very little cushion for challenges,
since petitioning takes a great deal of time. But Redler denotes new party
enrollees and tries to meet these voters, even though it often takes at least
three knocks on their doors until he finds these voters home. He noted
that he is often able to gather roughly twenty-five signatures in Bethlehem,
which is many more than needed to place a candidate on the ballot. And,
in doing so, he meets voters enrolled in his party.

Redler recounted that others told him belonging to the Working Families
Party prohibits him from voting in Democratic primary elections, since New
York operates under a closed primary system. He told me that by gathering
enough signatures for a candidate, he is able to produce several hundred
votes for that candidate. He observed that he was able to help candidates
win more votes at a general election by qualifying them to appear on the
Working Families Party ballot line through petitioning.

In addition to these subjects, I interviewed Andrew Falk of Putnam
County, another member of the Working Families Party state committee,
who works diligently on a number of policy issues that will be explained
elsewhere in this work. And Steven White of Rockland County expressed that
he sat on the steering committee for the Working Families Party in the past.

A noticeable portion of progressive activists are heavily involved in
the party structure of the Working Families Party by holding seats on its
state committee. And many are involved in various ways in granting their

party nomination to candidates seeking their line. But policy issues are also important, perhaps even independent of nominations for public office.

David Schwartz from Westchester County is a WFP state committee member and also the vice chair of the Westchester-Putnam chapter of the party. Through these positions, he concentrated on policy work. David Schwartz stated, "The Working Families Party, and I believe this is true, I think it's a very special place to put one's efforts because we use political power to achieve social, economic, and racial justice goals . . . and it seems pretty pure to me." He expressed that in eighteen years of being a party activist, he never observed anything other than party members working to achieve their policy goals.

The Working Families Party is clearly an issues-based party. And a large number of progressives spend a great deal of time advancing their efforts through a combination of electoral work and policy advocacy.

GREEN PARTY ENGAGEMENT

As mentioned at the very beginning of this book, there were a large number of Green Party enrollees casting ballots in a very competitive state committee race in 2000. I interviewed five subjects who are affiliated with the Green Party. Two of these individuals, Andrew Dalton and Dr. Barbara Kidney, held positions in the Hudson Valley chapter of the party. Dalton was the treasurer and Dr. Kidney was the cochair. Additionally, Dr. Kidney, during our interview, was running for state committee and was generous enough to talk to me in the middle of a very arduous process of tracking down over thirty Green Party members throughout Ulster County who were willing to sign a petition to place her name in nomination for a state committee seat. She was, indeed, successful in her task.

Both are engaged in campaigning for party nominees at every level of office. And Dr. Kidney used her position on the state committee to help state committee members think more dimensionally about their party platform.

Each and every Green Party activist is firm in their absolute commitment to peace. Each has been and is engaged in antiwar efforts, in many instances, going back over thirty years. Indeed, the research suggests antiwar, and antidrone activism is the hallmark of Green Party activity throughout the region, even more prominent than the commitment to environmentalism that is clearly personified in the Democratic and Working Families Parties as well. Further, a large part of their activism usually manifests itself through symbolic representation in the form of protests, rallies, and vigils.

The evidence from the interviews clearly illustrates that progressives are heavily involved in the structures of three political parties, holding seats in party organizations, recruiting people to be involved in party affairs, working to recruit candidates for public office, petitioning to qualify candidates for the ballot, and engaging in dialog about important policy issues. First, in the case of the Democratic Party, the endorsement of a committee implies that the committee will work to qualify you for the ballot, usually through designating petitions. As Craig Zumsteg told me, and as will be clarified later in the chapter, running for office is complicated, and the party members help a candidate obtain ballot status.

Second, should a candidate for public office wish to appear on a ballot line for a party other than the one in which they are enrolled, that candidate needs to be granted a certificate of authorization from the party whose nomination they are seeking (Schneider 2021). It is at the discretion of officials of the party in which the candidate is not enrolled to grant this certificate of nomination. As such, this is an important power for those in party offices to wield, largely because in many instances throughout state history, third-party lines often provided the margin of victory or defeat in an election.

Simply, the involvement of progressives in the party apparatus illustrates their robust presence in the Hudson Valley. It also illustrates how many work to use the government to achieve their goals. Further, more broadly, the research indicates that progressive activism is not only endemic to the city of New York, but progressives are denizens of urban, suburban, and rural areas outside of America's largest municipalities. You can find them in urban cities like Hudson and Albany. You can find them in suburban towns like Bethlehem. You can find them in sparsely populated regions of Greene County. And they engage in many other electoral efforts.

Campaigns and Elections

Progressives are involved in each stage of a campaign. They register voters and create a structure for parties to be successful in between campaigns. They work on candidate recruitment and training, ballot access, campaign strategy, and get-out-the-vote operations. They also run for public office and use their positions to achieve their goals. And they coordinate with other campaigns to find volunteers. Indeed, progressives have a robust and important presence in the electoral arena.

Voter Registration Efforts

Progressives spend a great deal of time registering voters and particular groups of voters. These activists have a noticeable role in helping others exercise the franchise.

Ginny O'Brien of Rensselaer County proclaimed, "I've been involved politically now with groups in terms of registering people for the 2020 elections . . . I made a vow to myself that I will not be a bystander, will not look the other way. I'm getting involved in doing everything I can to change the direction of the country right now." Maria Quackenbush of Dutchess County explained that most registration drives she has been part of, even with the Sanders campaign, occurred in middle-class areas. Maria noted that she registered voters in gyms and farmers markets. And she was deeply concerned about registering voters from more diverse backgrounds who are not actively sought after by many political activists.

Maria explained that she wished to focus registration efforts on peo-ple who are often ignored by politicos, including "millennials . . . people of color, the poor, the single moms . . ." She told me of the efforts of her husband, who also gave his time to this project, Michael Quackenbush. Maria explained that Michael spent a great deal of time in the lobby of the Family Partnership in Poughkeepsie, a nonprofit that works with many people of few economic means. Maria observed that during the Sanders campaign in 2016, they were able to register almost two hundred voters, sitting for roughly two hours a week. Sitting exactly where they were the following summer, Michael was only able to register two people who changed addresses. Maria recalled, "And because Trump was in office, and Bernie had lost, some of these people were so discouraged they said why bother and refused to register to vote." Michael Quackenbush told me about his time registering voters and plans for future efforts.

Michael articulated that his efforts to register voters were curtailed following the 2016 nominating process. He professed that voters said that, with the nominees being Donald Trump and Hillary Clinton, "there is no choice. There's simply nobody to vote for. It's not even the lesser of two evils. There's simply nobody to vote for." As for future efforts, Michael told me that his plans include going door to door in some of the poorest areas of the city of Poughkeepsie. He told me that he plans to go door to door on Main Street. Maria agreed, explaining that they hope to take clipboards and simply walk up and down Main Street or go and stand at Walmart to register voters. She hopes that these efforts show residents of these areas that, at the very least, progressives are trying to speak with these voters, noting that this connection is often vital. Progressives are not just trying to register voters who are from impoverished areas. They also pay attention to other groups who have been discriminated against.

Dr. Charles Chesnavage of Westchester recounted his efforts to register Muslim Americans to vote. Charles asserted voter registration of Muslim voters is a major part of his organization's mission. He told me that reaching out to the Muslim community has shifted the dynamics of elections for Yonkers City Council and other contests in Westchester County. As such, progressives engage in general voter registration efforts, while also paying attention to the poor and those from minority groups. Indeed, they have a robust presence in the Hudson Valley, outside of the metropolis of New York City, and use government and nonprofits to fight the status quo in efforts to advance equity and equal opportunity.

Progressives are also engaged in registering voters with two homes in New York at their Hudson Valley addresses. This tradition goes back to at least 1956, when Putnam County Republicans and then New York Attorney General Jacob Javits worked to disqualify several hundred voters in Putnam Valley who moved their voting addresses to their second homes in Putnam County from elsewhere in the state (Liberal Party Records 1956). After losing in the appellate term of the state supreme court, Javits did not appeal the decision to the state's highest court, the New York Court of Appeals (Liberal Party Records 1956a). As such, in 1956, due to the work of left-of-center activists in Putnam County, voters with multiple residences in New York, who are residents of the state, were afforded the "absolute right to select one of them as a permanent voting domicile" (Liberal Party Records 1956). Over sixty years later, progressive activists in the Hudson Valley work to tell voters about this particular right, and they reregister voters at their Hudson Valley addresses.

Jonathan Gross from rural Greene County highlighted his efforts to register voters. Gross told me about the background of the political dynamics of Greene County. He explained that there is a small core group of large political families who are Republicans, and these families come out and vote as a bloc. He told me that registering second homeowners in the county is a way to level the playing field, and they do so regularly. Another Greene County activist, Ellen Schorsch, upon my question about how important the second homeowner registration effort is, affirmed that often the difference between winning or losing a town position is a matter of two votes.

Ellen revealed that they do not seek to register all second homeowners. Instead, they focus on New York City areas with a heavy Democratic Party advantage like Brooklyn and Manhattan. She specifically stated that they do not seek to register people with residences in Rockland County or Long Island, where elections are more competitive. Schorsch noted that she works to register voters roughly every other week and targets areas where there are likely to be second homeowners. Ellen noted that she had distributed about two hundred applications to individuals in Greene County and hypothesized that about 80 percent of second homeowners she worked to register in Greene County changed their registrations. She noted, "I see these people afterwards and they say 'yeah we did it, we voted in our local election' . . . I'm very honest with them. I don't just try and hand out the applications. I talk to every single person and talk about the pros and cons and legalities. And this area happens to have a ton of second homeowners." Progressive activists in other counties also work to register second homeowners in the Hudson Valley.

Jen Fuentes of Ulster County told me that registering second homeowners from New York City is a strategy that local Democratic Party activists are using, because these votes are consistent in supporting the party. Fuentes professed that these second homeowners are found throughout the Hudson Valley—in Columbia, Greene, and Ulster Counties—and enrolling these voters at their second homes is "one of the ways in which the Democrats are finally getting their foot in the door." Lin Sakai, another Ulster County Democratic activist, told me about the "second homeowners campaign" that has been well received by party activists and is implemented by volunteers in the Hudson Valley and in New York City. The methods for implementing the campaign include postcards and phone calls. Sakai also gave me a dimensional explanation of how progressive activists work to register second homeowners in the Hudson Valley.

Sakai, noting the astute nature of the people organizing the campaign, explained that progressives examine property tax and voter registration documents and then determine who they can approach about registering in the Hudson Valley. Sakai noted that through their canvassing, calling, and postcarding efforts, they convinced three hundred voters to switch their registrations to the Hudson Valley. Sakai was delighted about this accomplishment. Dustin Reidy of Albany also shed light on the process. He explained that in New York's nineteenth congressional district there are around forty thousand individuals who own property in the district but hold voter registrations in New York City. Reidy explained, "We got the list of the Democrats. We postcarded, phone banked them, had a website, and registered about five hundred dual-resident voters."

As such, progressive activists are working to register voters in three ways: First, wide nets are generally cast to register as many voters as possible for the sake of increasing their civic engagement. Second, progressives work to enroll voters who are generally not approached by politicos, or those who are marginalized in some way, in order to give these groups power. Finally, progressives endeavor to register New York voters with two homes at their Hudson Valley addresses in order to increase the number of left-of-center voters in the region.

The data clearly illustrate that there is a robust progressive presence in the Hudson Valley, including in rural and suburban areas. And they seek to use government and their nonprofit groups to fight the status quo in order to advance their preferred policies.

RECRUITMENT AND TRAINING

Candidate recruitment happens both in and out of the party structure. John Schwartz, a Democratic committee town chair in Ulster County, articulates that through his position he helps candidates learn about the administrative hurdles to run for office, including gathering and filing petition signatures. Schwartz observed that town committees are a depository of "institutional knowledge," and it is their job to find candidates for public office and ask them to run in an election. He notes that this is a long process, and candidates need to be approached over a period of time. Mark Lieberman of Westchester made known that he is trying to encourage someone to run for council in Yorktown the year following our interview, because of how hard it is to find people to seek local offices. Other activists told me more stories about candidate recruitment.

Kamal Johnson—alderman of the city of Hudson at the time of our interview—said, "So, I started out running alone and then we brought in kind of like-minded candidates, and people who had a passion for politics and community." He noted that his efforts resulted in an entire slate of candidates, each and every one of whom won their primary elections.

Dr. Gregory Julian explained that progressives worked diligently in the 2017 General Election to convince a candidate to run for county executive, as no one else sought the position. He stated that progressives had an "absolute commitment to find a candidate." Dr. Julian observed that they were able to win the support of the Rockland County Democratic Chair at the time and that the progressive movement in the Rockland Democratic Party was the chief recruiter in finding a county executive candidate that year. Dr. Julian was also involved with candidate recruitment on a more microlevel.

He recalled that he and other progressives saw that candidates were not being recruited to run for local positions in the village of Suffern. Dr. Julian explained that the progressive movement worked diligently to find candidates, in particular for village trustee positions. And progressives also support efforts of nongovernmental organizations to recruit candidates for office.

Marjorie Hsu of Westchester told me, "I was particularly instrumental in setting up a fundraiser for an organization called Run for Something . . . Their basic premise is to find young, diverse progressives who would run for hyperlocal offices." Marjorie recounted that the founders hoped to convince around one hundred candidates to seek local offices nationwide but, instead, found that they successfully persuaded around fifteen hundred candidates to run. She noted that Run For Something collaborates with other organizations, including EMILYs List, to seek out, educate, and help these candidates win.

In New York it is extraordinarily complicated to run for office. Progressives are involved in helping potential candidates address and overcome the barriers to entry. A number of subjects explained difficulties with funding campaigns and gaining ballot access. Anthony Grice observed that it is extremely difficult for people without financial means to run for office, and he noted that a candidate who is not either middle class or upper-middle class often faces great difficulties. Grice continued, noting that in a political unit of roughly thirty thousand citizens, even sending a mailing to five thousand voters is still expensive. Additionally, yard signs, phone banking, hosting events, and get-out-the-vote operations also do not come free. Grice was not the only subject who talked about the expense of running for office.

London Reyes, who ran for Westchester Board of Legislators, observed: "Getting elected . . . it's a game . . . There's a system in place. It's all about numbers. And whoever has the most money, nine times out of ten, gets elected because they can send five or six mailers to a person's house. Who could afford that if you're a community person that's actually doing the work, right?" He noted that he was outspent by his opponents by seven dollars to one and asserted that his one mailer to voters cost over $3,000. It's also a costly and onerous effort to get on the ballot.

Nick Mottern of Westchester told me about his Democratic primary campaign against Rep. Nita Lowey in 1990. Mottern recounted that a local Democratic Party official told him bluntly that they will challenge his petitions and he will not make it onto the ballot. This did not deter Mottern from seeking a ballot spot. Mottern explained that the Democratic Party challenged enough signatures to prevent him from entering the primary. He stressed that it was not Republicans who challenged him, but Democrats. Mottern recalled his suit in federal court to be put on the ballot. Mottern explained, "The judge was quite sympathetic actually, and he said well, looking this over you don't have enough signatures, but I will let you refile your suit to oblige the Board of Elections in New York State to get clear written instructions to the public about what's necessary in terms of gathering signatures and otherwise to improving access to the ballot." Yet, Mottern lamented that he did not refile, which would have taken significant time and effort. He also expressed that incumbents know that onerous ballot access requirements protect them from challenges.

Steven Greenfield explained how the major parties use both onerous ballot access requirements and lack of campaign funds to stop challengers. Greenfield, a Green Party nominee for Congress in New York's nineteenth congressional district in 2018 and 2020, noted that state law determines the number of signatures required to achieve ballot status. In his case, as a Green, his petitions were challenged by the Democrats, which then requires hiring an election attorney, many of whom charge $300 an hour. Greenfield disclosed that he was successful in appearing on the ballot because he had pro bono attorneys. Greenfield stated that petition challenges often lead to completely depleting a campaign war chest and argued that parties have budget line items to challenge nominating petitions. He stated, "Even if those petition challenges fail, they bankrupt the candidate because everyone knows lawyers are really, really expensive." Thus, it is clear that New York has burdensome and litigious ballot qualification requirements.

And this is why progressives are so important in the ballot qualification process. They have been gathering petitions for years and provide the shoe leather and the expertise to successfully qualify candidates for office in a purposely onerous legal environment.

Dylan Basescu from Westchester County described his efforts to help a candidate obtain ballot status for municipal office. Dylan stated that he gathered roughly a quarter of the signatures necessary to qualify the candidate for the ballot. He noted that he is trained in the legal requirements of ballot access in the state. *Betty Danson* told me that she works with the

Voter Activation Network in *Yeovil*. In this role, she produces lists of voters from the network for campaigns in their petitioning efforts. *Betty* continued that she regenerated updated lists as needed, to account for those voters who already signed petitions. *She* reported that her efforts helped activists gather several hundred signatures for countywide candidates over a few weeks. Gathering signatures for the Democratic Party with a rich enrollment of members is one thing. Attempting to secure a third-party line, where there might only be a handful of enrollees in a given political unit, is far more difficult.

Craig Zumsteg, who told me one tale of his experiences in obtaining a signature of a third-party member, explained that gathering signatures is not without hazard. He recalled going to a house without a fence where a gigantic dog, who could hardly see due to cataracts, appeared and started barking zealously. Craig recounted, "And I just stood on the sidewalk and I waited for probably two and a half or three minutes until owners came out and then I told them what I was up to, and they invited me in" and then signed the petition. Zumsteg articulated that simply getting this signature so a candidate can appear on a third-party line was gratifying. Steve Redler, who is commissioned as a notary public, gathers petitions for his own party, the Working Families Party. He also collected signatures for the Independence Party when it held ballot status.

Redler collects petition signatures from Working Families Party enrollees in the town of Bethlehem, where he resides, but also in the neighboring town of Coeymans, as well as in Greene County. He noted that doing so takes a good deal of time on the road. Redler also explained that he worked on gathering signatures for the Independence Party, which he noted is a great deal of work. Indeed, petitioners seeking signatures from former enrollees of the Independence Party, which lost ballot status at the 2020 General Election, often had the difficult task of convincing voters that they were actually enrolled in a political party. Many former Independence Party members believed they were enrolling as political independents. Instead, these voters joined an actual political party but often did not believe volunteers gathering petitions that they were enrolled in a political party. And after party workers convinced voters that they belonged to a party, volunteers then had to persuade these voters to sign their nominating petitions.

Beyond local races, progressives also gather petitions for statewide candidates. John Gromada of Rockland chronicled his petition process for Cynthia Nixon and Jumaane Williams in their races against Andrew Cuomo and Kathy Hochul, respectively. For several years, due to quirks with election law, New York State held at least two different primary elections. A federal primary for US Senate and US House was held in June. State and local primaries took place in September. Gromada took advantage of this situation. He recalled that he collected signatures at a poll site on the day of the June Democratic primary for candidates seeking nomination in the September primary contest. Doing so, he was able to collect signatures of one hundred Democrats for Cynthia Nixon in her gubernatorial primary campaign. He explained that taking this approach was strategic, noting that every single person who left the polls was enrolled in the Democratic Party and politically engaged enough to cast ballots in a primary election, which obviously has a smaller turnout than the general election. Progressives work assiduously to make democracy happen. They are a driving force in qualifying candidates to appear on the ballot, not only helping individuals who might not know the process but also giving voters a choice in primary and general elections. But it is not just a matter of understanding costs and appearing on the ballot; progressives make other important contributions in preparing candidates to run for public office.

Craig Zumsteg made known that he is working to create an election consulting firm, or as he called it, "basically a campaign in a box." He declared that through this effort he endeavors to have an entity where a candidate can find all of the principles needed to run a campaign, such as graphic designers, fundraisers, campaign managers, among others. He observed that creating something like this would open the field to potential candidates who find the barriers to running impossible to overcome. Candidates have to face the realities of running for office, including getting on the ballot, raising funds, navigating legal requirements, developing messaging, and so forth. Zumsteg further observed that many candidates for local office in particular have jobs and other responsibilities that further prevent them from seeking office. He declared, "If you come in with a plug-and-play operation, all you need is the local talent, and you can change the entire pipeline on these things." Zumsteg's plan seems to fall outside of the party organizational structure. Other progressives help candidates through their party positions.

John Schwartz noted that a great deal of training and mentorship occurs in many professions. But he affirmed that individual party committees play a major role in helping candidates. He observed that party committees are repositories of knowledge and teach candidates how to run campaigns and win elections. More subjects told me about their training and recruitment activities.

Jen Fuentes annually organizes campaigns and elections training for the Ulster County Democratic Committee, where she educates people on running for office and offers a great many suggestions. Fuentes explained that she covers ballot access and developing a plan to run their campaigns. She also told me about the hurdles that New York election law places on candidates for public office who are not familiar with the intricacies of the law. *Steve Jones* told me that he is involved with the "Pipeline Project" that works to educate those not currently involved in politics, particularly young people, how to successfully seek public office. Steve Redler noted that the Working Families Party operates programs to help candidates running for public office. He noted that those running for offices like state senate often have some experiences in municipal races, but this school helps them sharpen their skills to seek these higher positions.

Carolyn Riggs exclaimed, "I found a love for organizing for Democrats in rural areas. So, a colleague and I started a local action committee called the Rural Majority Project this year. The Rural Majority Project's sole focus and mission is to elect Democrats in traditionally red and historically conservative communities." Riggs explained that this group finds candidates to run for office in places that usually do not have Democrats on the ballot and then educates and offers support to these candidates. In addition to candidates, the Rural Majority Project also helps Democratic committees increase their base, raise money, and find candidates to seek public office. Riggs noted that she was not aware of another organization engaging candidates and committees in the way that the Rural Majority Project does. As Riggs told us, the training she conducts is also for volunteers. Training volunteers is, indeed, something progressives place a premium on in rural, suburban, and urban parts of the Hudson Valley.

Lin Sakai of Ulster County noted that she has been talking with others for several years to develop "an infrastructure of training." Sakai envisions a training for volunteers and party activists at every level from occasional volunteers all the way through campaign managers. Sakai noted that in her opinion, progressives compose a movement that needs activists with different skills, and the first step is to find out what skill sets activists possess. She noted that once you find out the things people are good at performing and want to perform, you can recruit them to help. And Sakai noted that this is the first step. What comes next is convincing these volunteers to train in areas in which they are not yet comfortable, then give them the skills to become leaders in the movement. Other progressives work on training volunteers as well.

Craig Zumsteg recounted his efforts at a remote farmhouse, where he trained over one hundred volunteer canvassers in a day. Zumsteg recalled that he trained volunteers in different shifts on how to use the MiniVAN app. He recalled that he is able to give the same repeated presentation many times over and, in doing so, taught these volunteers software and how to canvass voters.

Shannon Powell explains why this is important. She asserted, "But at the heart of everything is electoral politics, because unless the right people get elected it doesn't matter what your issue is; it's not going anywhere." Powell continued that her primary guiding principle is that if there is the ability to help a campaign, one should help that campaign. Additionally, she noted that she believes it is helpful for volunteers themselves to be involved with campaign work since they gain valuable information through various training opportunities and workshops, such as how to participate in a text bank. Carolyn Guyer noted that seasoned political activists in her county ran workshops on how to canvass. Carolyn told me that these workshops taught basics of canvassing, including activities that canvassers should and should not do. This is important because progressives are out on the campaign trail campaigning for candidates at all levels of government in urban, suburban, and rural areas. And they bring people together to work on campaigns.

Indeed, this training clearly illustrates that there is a robust progressive presence in the region, outside of New York City. Further, many of these volunteers operate through nonprofit groups such as Indivisible or the political party structure in order to attempt to capture government. As Shannon Powell expressed, progressives need to elect individuals who will carry out their policy goals.

CAMPAIGNING AND CANVASSING

Carolyn Guyer told me about the importance of bringing in new volunteers to her area and the reaction of the local Democratic committees. She asserted that progressive canvassing efforts had an impact on local races. She also recalled that some local party committees were not canvassing previously and that local party officials, at first, were not sure what to do with these new volunteers.

Indeed, many volunteers find their way to unfamiliar turf. Dustin Reidy is the founder of NY19 Votes, a group whose purpose was to defeat former US Rep. John Faso. Reidy described the group's first canvass. He expressed, "From my background, my thought was if we are going to flip

Congress, which is what we need to do, and get John Faso out of office, we need to talk to voters early. Show all these newly energized activists how to talk to voters, how to canvass, how to register voters, and how to do that door to door." Reidy proclaimed that there were thirteen sites throughout the district to organize canvassers, and on the first day, over four hundred volunteers were out in the district engaging voters. Reidy also recalled that these canvassers spent many hours going door to door and enjoyed their experience. He noted that through his group's efforts, people who never campaigned before the first event of NY19 Votes quickly accepted new responsibilities and became leaders at canvass sites the following November. These efforts sent out sixty to seventy volunteers each day. Reidy documented the growth of many of these volunteers—who were initially hesitant to knock on doors—to become the organizers of campaigns over a short period of time. He observed, "That is like the best feeling in the world when I can say I played a small to large role in making that happen." Finally, he told me that his group, NY19 Votes, is given a great deal of credit for establishing an organizational structure of volunteers inside and outside of this rural district that eventually led to Antonio Delgado taking the seat from John Faso. Indeed, NY19 Votes played a large part in the 2018 Congressional Election. Others chronicled their experiences with NY19 Votes.

Lin Sakai also told me about the first canvass of NY19 Votes. She explained that Dustin Reidy called her and asked about her opinion of holding a "resistance canvass" during the month of March. She admitted that she thought it was a stretch due to the weather. Sakai told me that the canvass took place on an extremely cold day, and canvassers were knocking on doors to inquire about voters' opinions of Representative Faso not holding town hall meetings. Sakai recalled, in concert with Reidy, that many of the canvassers were new to this practice but enjoyed the experience. Sakai reported, "We ran a one-year campaign without a candidate. Because again, we wanted to keep spreading the word and just talk about just basic Democratic values."

Craig Zumsteg chronicled his experiences with volunteers using campaign technology. He recalled that using campaign technology, on a given Saturday, roughly thirty people would go out in a morning shift. While they are canvassing, they are inputting information into the application. Zumsteg continued, explaining that the second shift would show up roughly ninety minutes later, and that second shift of canvassers would go to the doors of people that were not home for the first wave of canvassers. He revealed that the same thing would happen with the third wave of canvassers. The application would send them to the houses where the first and second shifts reported that no one was home. Zumsteg proudly told me, "Highland is an area that never had that sort of attention before. And now we're sending six waves a weekend through . . . hitting every door."

Zumsteg offered a dimensional overview of how they engaged voters. He explained that canvassers would engage voters with local candidates first, beginning with the Democratic nominee for Ulster county sheriff, Juan Figueroa. He noted that if voters were receptive to Figueroa, volunteers would tell them about Pat Strong, who was running for state senate. And, if they were still interested, then volunteers would talk about Antonio Delgado, the party's congressional nominee. But progressives do not just campaign in even-numbered years. They work continuously.

Lin Sakai asserted that it is of the utmost importance to continue to speak with voters and it was her plan to keep doing so regardless of the results of the 2018 General Election. Sakai observed that these volunteers recruited from her and Reidy's efforts were appreciated and accepted by the local Democratic committees, who were undergoing changes. And the result was wins for Democrats in many towns in Ulster County, which Sakai claimed was a success. She reported, "But the point is that process of again, finding the people, training the people, so they could train the trainers." Lin Sakai described the importance of bringing together activists inside and outside of the party structure.

She recounted that her county committee chair endorsed NY19 Votes and their efforts, stating that it was not the job of the county chair to hinder their undertakings. And she argued that it was their goal to simply win majorities on town boards. Sakai also noted that NY19 Votes produced a model for winning local majorities that had all of the working parts needed for Democrats to win locally. Lin was not the only person canvassing without a candidate.

Tom Denton of Ulster County told me about Olive Action, a local group of activists who helped pull out over 85 percent of votes in local elections through what he called the Neighbor-to-Neighbor plan. Denton explained that Neighbor-to-Neighbor is based on relationships developed among neighbors in a given area, such as the town of Olive. Developing these relationships is a way to cultivate votes. Denton articulated that the program clearly works, as Olive was able to achieve a mammoth voter turnout. And so the Neighbor-to-Neighbor plan is being developed in other places in the Hudson Valley, including rural, suburban, and urban areas.

Betty Danson provided more information on Neighbor-to-Neighbor. *Betty* made known that volunteers canvass for a total of twelve hours each year and visit the same houses each and every time. *Betty* noted that volunteers typically visit thirty houses in their neighborhoods. She explained that the first time a volunteer visits a neighbor, they inquire as to what neighbors are thinking, in order to begin the Neighbor-to-Neighbor relationship and become acquainted with the voters. Then, volunteers go out prior to the primary and general elections. *Betty* then told me that volunteers are then able to go out and use a voter application to help gather petitions, and that this application is also helping with canvassing during special elections. Progressives in other parts of the region also spent a great deal of time canvassing.

Shannon Powell from Westchester reported that her group's first large endeavor was a canvass in the spring of 2017 following her group's formation. Powell articulated the importance of educating activists and volunteers through canvassing. Shannon joyfully said, "Now people are addicted to canvassing . . . and now they're like experts . . . they're the ones who go canvass in a heartbeat." When I asked about the point of this first canvass, Powell explained it was to let people know about the upcoming election for Westchester County Executive. The incumbent, at the time, was a supporter of Donald Trump. Powell told me that the Democrats did not even have a candidate at the time of the first canvass, but people were canvassing throughout Westchester. Powell observed that education and empowerment are the important factors. The success of Westchester progressives in 2017, and their canvassing, continued into the 2018 midterm.

Powell recounted that in 2018 they were helping four state senate nominees and two US representative candidates. Of this group, Peter Harckham, Jen Metzger, Antonio Delgado, and Anthony Brindisi won their races. Powell recalled that they used opportunities to campaign for multiple candidates at the same time, since state senate and congressional lines overlap. So, volunteers can campaign for more than one candidate at the same time. Indivisible volunteers also campaigned for Anthony Brindisi in his congressional race, even though the district is outside of the Hudson Valley. According to Shannon, Indivisible Westchester sent a bus to the city of Binghamton on two consecutive weekends and canvassed 1,200 doors. Brindisi won the election by just under 4,500 votes (New York State Board of Elections 2018).

Progressives bring activists together in other ways. Connie Hogarth, a longtime progressive currently based in Dutchess County, often opens her home to bring people together for political purposes. She reported that she and another friend founded a group called Take 18 in 2005, whose aim was to elect a Democrat in New York's eighteenth congressional district.

She revealed that activists have been meeting in her home monthly since 2005 to talk about policy and meet candidates for office. Progressives are also involved in other coordinated campaign efforts as well.

Shannon Powell reported that in Rob Astorino's initial race for Westchester County Executive in 2009, he argued "eight years is enough" for a person to be county executive. Powell told me about efforts to unseat Astorino in 2017. She proclaimed, "We had a team that just basically bird-dogged him . . . We went and showed up at every town hall he had, every debate." Powell recounted that at the time, Astorino ushered in rules changes that allowed him to seek a third term. Powell told me that her group projected his quote on buildings that he was campaigning in and an activist would dress up in a chicken suit because Astorino refused to debate his opponent. Clearly, progressives also know how to have fun on the campaign trail.

It is apparent that progressives are involved in every stage of a campaign. And that these campaigns occur in rural, suburban, and urban parts of the Hudson Valley, and even in areas adjacent to the region. They help recruit candidates. They work to qualify candidates for the ballot. They talk to voters throughout the campaign and may even do so without a candidate running. And they have fun assisting candidates in other ways, even dressing in the occasional chicken suit. They are also an important force at the end of the campaign, working to get out the vote.

Carolyn Guyer explained her get-out-the-vote efforts. This included contacting people about their registration status and creating literature to educate citizens about early voting and other election law changes that New York passed over the last few years. Guyer revealed that this civic education is important so high school students can learn that they are able to preregister to vote, or that employers are legally obligated to give their workers three hours of time to vote, with pay. Steven White also works to mobilize voters. He created what he called "a communication media device called *Power of Ten*." It works on the notion that if every activist convinced ten people to vote, and then each of those ten persuaded another ten citizens to vote, and then each of those ten induced another ten citizens—this would spark ten thousand people to vote. While he was not victorious in his own campaign where he created this system, his medium still publishes several times each month. Finally, as political activists know, lists of voters and their contact information is a valued form of political currency. Steven White observed that because he had roughly six thousand people who subscribe to Power of Ten, he has gained political influence in the county. Simply, activists know that he has six thousand readers that he can influence. As such, progressives are a key part of the democratic process throughout the Hudson Valley. It is not hyperbole to argue that they help make elections happen. They give voters a choice at the ballot box.

Progressives work to capture government and use nonprofit vehicles such as Take 18 and Indivisible to fight the status quo. And this narrative reveals that they are interested in advancing equity and equal opportunity by paying attention to individuals who have been ignored, educating people about their rights, or using their position to elect candidates who will fight for equity and equal opportunity. Further, their activism takes place in rural, suburban, and urban areas of the region. This was also important in their campaigns against members of the Independent Democratic Conference.

Campaigning Against the Independent Democratic Conference

Many progressive activists spoke about primary battles against local members of the former Independent Democratic Conference (IDC) of the New York state senate. The IDC was a small group of state senators, elected as Democrats, who shared power with the Republicans in the state senate. This allowed the Republicans to stay in the majority, even though more Democrats were elected to the chamber.

Shannon Powell told me about her support for Alessandra Biaggi, in her victorious quest to wrestle the Democratic Party nomination from Senator Jeff Klein. Supporting Biaggi included organizing a fundraiser and coordinating members of her group to volunteer for Biaggi. Susan Van Dolsen explained that her group coordinated with the Communications Workers of America to phone bank for candidates, including Biaggi.

Former State Senator Jeff Klein was not the only target of Hudson Valley progressives. In Rockland County, activists worked to defeat David Carlucci, an IDC state senator. Dr. Gregory Julian observed that progressives were spearheading the plan to recruit a candidate to challenge Carlucci in the Democratic primary. Gina I. noted that they worked diligently to keep the importance of challenging Carlucci relevant over several months and were in contact with several potential candidates to launch a primary campaign against Carlucci. Gina I. noted that many potential candidates were intimidated by Carlucci's large campaign war chest. In early May, progressives found a candidate willing to challenge Carlucci. Gina I. recalled, "I think she is super smart . . . she knows the issues. She understands the district, you know, what the different forces are. And we're doing it." Gina told me that Rockland Citizens Action Network, as well as other activists not affiliated with the group, organized the candidate's campaign. And that candidate's name is Julie Goldberg, who contributed time to this study.

John Gromada explained his efforts to inform voters about the Independent Democratic Conference. This work included writing news releases and coordinating Goldberg's social media presence. Additionally, Gromada organized fundraisers that included Broadway stars and gathered petition signatures to qualify Goldberg for the ballot. Finding a candidate to run against Senator David Carlucci was not easy.

When I spoke to Julie Goldberg, she noted the difficult time that Carlucci's opponents had finding a candidate. She told me that she offered to be a candidate if progressives could not find anyone else to run. Julie, who is a practicing librarian, initially became involved in the effort to defeat Carlucci by offering to conduct research. But as no candidate emerged, Julie told me that it would be demoralizing to progressive activists if no challenger would agree to run. That said, she ran because no one else would commit to doing so. Julie asserted that if no one ran, there would be no consequences for an elected official that many people feel deceived them. Julie noted that most people who worked for her worked for Senator Carlucci at some point. Upon her losing the primary with a respectable 46.10 percent of the vote, she stated that Carlucci "voted exactly as I would have" in the following term, and that "we didn't change senators; we changed the senator" (Rockland County Board of Elections 2018).

Jacquelyn Drechsler of Rockland County, who observed that the IDC prevented a great deal of policy from being realized, believes that progressives changed Carlucci's behavior through this primary. Drechsler noted that Carlucci has, over his career, done a great many good things for her county, including for mental health issues. Drechsler lamented, "But he's also, by his actions, blocking money for the East Ramapo schools, blocking many different things that needed to be moved forward out of committee, and they weren't moving forward because they would be blocked by the IDC. So, we didn't have the victory, but I think we may have contributed a little bit to that change." Indeed, for progressive activists in Westchester and Rockland Counties, working to defeat Independent Democratic state senators in primaries took much of their time.

In the case of defeating Jeff Klein, progressives saw a clear victory. And while Julie Goldberg did not win her nominating contest against David Carlucci, she and Jacquelyn Drechsler noted that progressives changed the incumbent's behavior. As such, their participation and their presence mattered. It is important to note that these campaigns illustrate a strong progressive presence in the various geographies of the Hudson Valley. Further, and this is clearly evident by Drechsler's statements, they fought the status quo in hopes of advancing equity and equal opportunity, such as money for the East Ramapo School District that was being blocked by the majority in the state senate.

Julie Goldberg was not the only progressive to run for office in the Hudson Valley. Indeed, a great many activists sought and/or hold public office.

Progressives Run for Office

Progressives endeavor to become elected officials. This has been noted in much of the writing so far. Some run knowing that they will not be victorious. Others run to win but do not get elected. And some are triumphant in their first contests. This section will explore why progressives seek public office in rural, suburban, and urban parts of the Hudson Valley.

Andrew Zink of Ulster County told me that one of the reasons he was encouraged to run for the county legislature was due to the way Bernie Sanders was treated by the Democratic Party, which Zink believed needed to change. Zink explained that he decided to run in an extremely Republican district, where he did not have a good chance of winning, and his town did not even have an active Democratic committee. Zink recalled that his opponent did not even have a challenger in the previous election. Zink told me, "I just felt that I had to stand up and I had to do something . . . I want to look back one day and know that I did everything that I could." Finally, through the process, the town's Democratic Party became active again. Others shared stories about choosing to give voters a choice.

Dr. Gregory Julian revealed that he ran in 2008 for state senate against longtime incumbent Tom Morahan. Dr. Julian explained that he attended a Martin Luther King Day Parade in the state of Florida in 2008, and there were volunteers for Senator Obama campaigning at the event. Dr. Julian recounted, "I felt like I felt when Kennedy was running." He observed that they were not campaigning effectively, so he approached them and gave them direction about how to more effectively hand out literature as a team. He declared that at that moment, he became an "Obama activist." Dr. Julian asserted that the core of his supporters came from women and prochoice activists, as he was an advisory board member for Planned Parenthood. Dr. Julian explained that he knew he was not going to win the election, but his goal was to encourage women activists to become engaged in the Rockland

County political arena. It is clear that candidates for public office run for reasons other than winning.

Connie Hogarth, when asked if she ever ran for office, told me about her state assembly campaign in the 1970s. She declared that she campaigned on ending the war in Vietnam, banning the death penalty, securing a woman's right to choose, and closing Indian Point Energy Center. Hogarth noted that she was not running to win, but to bring attention to her platform issues. And Connie told me that she was grateful to not win, as she could not see how she could have done what she did over the past fifty years if she needed to be in Albany a great deal of the time. Others run to win an election, even when they are not victorious.

Andrew Falk of Putnam County explained, "If you don't have anybody standing up and fighting . . . it's never going to get better . . . I'm sick and tired of rich people running for office as a vanity play. And I had every opportunity growing up. I just want, you know, selfishly, I want my kids to have every opportunity that I had growing up. But really, it's about all kids and then grandkids." Falk asked several questions during the interview. He wanted to know about the shrinking of the middle class and disappearance of opportunities and union jobs. And he noted that someone needs to fight in order to ameliorate these issues. Falk ran competitive races for state assembly in 2012 and 2014 (New York State Board of Elections 2012; New York State Board of Elections 2014a).

And, in 2015, he ran for supervisor of the town of Patterson in Putnam County where he lost by just 17 votes out of 1,948 ballots cast (Putnam County Board of Elections 2015). Falk recalled that he ran for supervisor because of the plan to privatize the town sanitation department, staffed by Civil Service Employees Association members, one of New York's most prominent public sector unions. Falk told me that sanitation workers asked him to run due to his track record on labor issues, noting that they would lose their jobs if the department was privatized. Falk remembered how tired he was at the time, but he simply could not ignore the sanitation workers. Falk told me that he spoke to a consultant who warned him that the town was heavily Republican in its voting pattern and registration. He noted that the consultant gave him a 30 percent chance of victory. Falk affirmed, "Well, I'm not going to let facts get in the way of doing what's right . . . I spent months and months and months just knocking, knocking on every door of every voter that was likely to vote in 2015. And I lost that election by seventeen votes; I should never have come close."

Falk recounted that he was not able to be involved with get-out-the-vote efforts because he suffered a heart attack three days before Election Day. He also wanted to check himself out of the hospital against doctor's orders. Falk remembered, "And I knew what I was going to say to the press . . . 'When Andy Falk gets a heart attack, the heart attack dies.'" But the press never asked him for a statement. Falk told me that he organized an endeavor to encourage people to attend a town board meeting and speak in favor of not privatizing the sanitation department. His efforts resulted in three hundred people attending a meeting that had to be moved to a bigger location. The meeting was the first time he went out since his heart attack. Ultimately, the town voted to keep the department public and has since put more money into it. He extolled, "I'm very, very, very happy to be in a little piece of that." Andrew Falk was not the only progressive to seek office multiple times for good reasons.

Kat Brezler highlighted her multiple runs for public office. She sought local office in Yonkers because she believed that the city needed an independent school district, an elected school board, and more local representation and transparency in city government. Several years later, she recalled another race in White Plains where she ran for city council to work toward affordable housing and to "give the working class a break from ticketing, because parking tickets in White Plains become a micro-tax on the working class." Regarding her election for state senate, Brezler explained her campaign focused on single-payer healthcare, cannabis, and rights for tenants. Kat Brezler was not the only subject who ran for office in Westchester.

Terence Miller told me that he ran for city council in Yonkers so he could exercise power on behalf of those who have been ignored by government. He was interested in helping those left behind. He observed that constituents in his district hoped for reform and focused on communicating his messaging to these constituents. Miller lamented that his opponents raised more money and he was simply not able to reach voters in the way he hoped. Yet, he acknowledged that he still was competitive in the election. The call to duty seems to be a continuing theme in explaining why progressives run for office.

Pramilla Malick noted that she ran after realizing that elected officials were simply corrupt or complacent and "this entire community and county . . . was being sacrificed. I knew that the only way to defend the county and community was to run for office myself." Malick recalled that she saw firsthand how the Platform Committee of the Democratic National

Committee, which was supposed to bring Sanders supporters into the party structure in 2016, simply did not care about issues that directly impact Americans. Malick explained that Sanders's supporters wanted the Democratic National Committee to adopt a plank to ban fracking due to its detrimental impact to public health. Malick said she "witnessed so many games, so much trickery, so much deception, and I realized that these people are not honest brokers." Malick concluded that the platform committee was simply influenced by the fracking companies and was not interested in public health. Again, candidates ran because of issues that lead to fighting the status quo in support of equity and equal opportunity.

Pat Strong of Ulster County ran for New York state senate in 2018; it was her first campaign for public office. She told me that she never thought about seeking office before the Ulster County Young Democrats made known that Republican Senator George Amedore needed a challenger. Strong explained that her platform focused on a number of progressive issues that the Republican majority in the New York state senate would either vote down or simply not address. Strong also unsuccessfully sought the Democratic nomination for Ulster County Executive in 2019.

One of my subjects ran in the past as a Republican. Kim Izzarelli of Westchester told me, "Well, I'm really honestly scared of what's going on right now. I genuinely care; I have a nineteen-year-old daughter and a twenty-one-year-old son." She made known that she ran for village board, town board, and the state assembly as a Republican, as well as school board, which is nonpartisan. She recounted that her initial interest in running for office focused on fiscal issues, like budgeting and spending, as well as advocating for small government. This initially started in 2008, around the fiscal crisis. But Izzarelli cares about other issues as well; she is prochoice, and protecting a woman's right to choose is a chief concern for her.

Steven Greenfield was the Green Party nominee who ran for Congress in New York's nineteenth congressional district in 2018 and 2020. Greenfield believes that votes are not guaranteed, but candidates should earn votes. He also noted that there was not an overlap of a single issue between his campaign platform and Delgado's platform. When people levied charges that he was taking votes away from the Democratic nominee, which would elect a Republican in the district, Greenfield argued that there would need to be overlap in their platforms for the Green Party nominee to take votes away from the Democratic Party nominee. He noted, "Nobody ever looks at Delgado's website and says, oh he's providing just a better version of the Republican platform . . . he'll be siphoning votes away from Republicans.

That sounds comical to even suggest that." So, Greenfield ran to differentiate himself from other candidates, including Antonio Delgado, the Democrat.

Other progressives were not successful in their initial runs for office but were victorious in later elections. Anthony Grice told me that a neighbor of his encouraged him to run for over roughly a ten-year period, even though he had no intention of becoming a candidate. Grice stated that a friend called him to let him know that a municipal legislative seat was open in his district. Grice recounted that he had a history of community engagement that focused on a number of policy concerns that he hoped his municipality could pursue. Still, Grice did not immediately decide to run.

At the party committee meeting that followed the phone call, Grice introduced himself as a candidate for the open seat. He then explained that another local politician also announced that he was running for the same seat. Grice did not withdraw from the contest and ran an issue-oriented, respectful, positive campaign. He noted that he lost that race but received a respectable amount of votes. After the election, he was immediately involved again in community affairs. He noted that a municipality-wide legislative position opened midterm and he was appointed to fill it by sitting legislators, including the legislator that he ran against in the previous general election.

Grice observed, "I think that spoke to my character and theirs. That they knew that, 'Hey, here's an upstanding guy that even in the election, he didn't play dirty politics. He did his research. He stood for what he believed in, and he was respectful about it.'" He continued that the legislators gave him a chance to serve. Grice was then elected to the position twice after his appointment.

Another progressive activist, Linda Mussmann, current county supervisor in Hudson's Fourth Ward, told me about her various runs for public office. Her first run for office, which was for the mayor of the city of Hudson, came about because of a corporation endeavoring to construct a cement plant in Hudson. She recalled that the plant caused her and a number of activists to become engaged in the electoral arena. Mussmann recounted the process of obtaining her ballot line, the Bottom Line Party. She told me she learned a great deal about the complicated procedures of circulating and filing independent nominating petitions in New York, the mechanism to form a ballot line in a given election. Mussmann also recounted learning how to campaign and interact with voters. Explaining her campaign strategy, Mussmann told me, "I wanted to go and knock on people's doors and say, 'Hi, I'm Linda Mussmann. I'm running for mayor and I would like to talk to you about how I see things possible for Hudson, and particularly about the cement plant being something that was not going to be a positive for our community because it was being built right at the top of the city.' " As we mentioned in other parts of this chapter, running for office in New York is not easy.

Mussmann revealed that cement plant supporters viewed her entry into the race as a threat to the project, as both Democrats and Republicans supported the plant. She explained that during this campaign New York still used mechanical lever voting machines. And, in most areas outside of New York City, parties were listed from top to bottom on the machine. Her Bottom Line Party actually appeared on the bottom of the ballot, below all of the other parties; as such, this made it easy for voters to find her name. Mussmann noted that the Bottom Line Party became so popular that her opponent in the following election circulated his own petitions to run on the Bottom Line Party. Mussmann explained that this opponent filed his papers before she did and claimed the Bottom Line Party. In that contest, Mussmann appeared on the ballot as the "Third Deal Party" candidate. Mussmann was elected the county supervisor for Hudson's Fourth Ward in 2017 (Columbia County Board of Elections 2017).

Another progressive was also not successful in her first race but later won office. Ginny O'Brien of Rensselaer told me that she ran because she was engaged in the community as a parent and seeking public office seemed like a logical progression, and that she had a keen interest in town affairs. She recalled she was unsuccessful in her first quest for office, running against an incumbent town clerk. O'Brien noted that her unsuccessful contest likely helped her to gain name recognition, which was useful as she was success-ful in a quest for town board four years later. O'Brien observed that she beat an incumbent in her initial town board race and then was reelected. O'Brien stated, "And I enjoyed it; I really liked being on the town board."

Other candidates ran and won in their first campaigns. *Steve Jones* recalled that after he retired, he read that the county legislature decreased nonprofit funding in the middle of the year, while also giving themselves a salary increase. He continued, "And it just didn't sit right with me that they would vote themselves a pay increase and cut nonprofit organization funding midyear." *Jones* noted that his wife thought he should run for county legislator. He recalled that he never thought to seek office before, but he ran. And, in an extremely Republican district, *Jones* won by less than one hundred votes in his first race and was reelected by a much smaller margin in his second race.

Kamal Johnson, who was elected mayor of the city of Hudson in 2019, was an alderman at the time of our conversation. When I asked

Kamal why he sought office initially, he recounted that the debilitated state of the youth center in the city of Hudson was the issue that sparked his interest. He noted that the infrastructure of the building was run down and they could not fund programs at the center. Johnson recalled that he advocated for the center at council meetings and offered to help the center voluntarily. Johnson remembered, "And they will always tell me, you have great ideas . . . but you're not at the table. And there's a process to certain things." Johnson made clear that he saw his words were not moving council members: "So, I got to the table." He recalled that people did not think he was a viable candidate in his ward due to demographics and his status as a political novice at the time. But, through his campaign, he was able to produce a large voter turnout and win. As such, Johnson was able to win two elections in Hudson.

Dr. Maria May, who was elected a town board member after our interview, asserted that she started to observe that there was subterfuge in her local government after she started attending their meetings. Dr. May recalled, "We have a big land parcel . . ." and several elected officials were "being very opaque about what is being done with that parcel." Indeed, Dr. May was elected to the town board in her first run for office.

Several subjects knew that they would not win their elections. They used their nominations to highlight policy solutions to particular problems. Others hoped to win their contests in order to advance policies that they believed would help to bring about equity and equal opportunity. No subject appeared to seek office for personal gain or achievement. Indeed, their interviews suggest they ran in order to advance policy solutions, even if their races only brought attention to issues that they thought should garner wider public consideration. All that said, it is very clear by the particular manner of how these progressives entered the electoral arena that there is a robust progressive presence in rural, suburban, and urban parts of the Hudson Valley. It follows then, that progressives are actively engaged in the political arena outside of America's largest municipalities. And these activists endeavor to use government and nonprofit organizations to fight the status quo to advance equity and equal opportunity.

Conclusion

Progressives are a key part of the organizational structures of the Democratic, Working Families, and Green Parties. I interviewed members of each of the state committees of these parties. For the Democrats, a number of progressive activists are also elected to county committee seats, which ensures them a position on their town or city Democratic committees. Progressives encourage others to run for party positions while also leveraging their party posts to impact general elections.

They hold party office, recruit and train candidates and volunteers, organize canvasses, coordinate within the progressive movement and party structure, and get out the vote. They phone and text bank, write postcards, host fundraisers and meet and greets, give money, distribute literature, put up signs, and write press releases and social media posts. They are an integral part of the ballot qualification process, gathering signatures and filing caucus paperwork to ensure that candidates for office qualify to appear on the ballot. And they may even have fun in the process, employing the occasional chicken suit to help a candidate win.

In particular, the amount of time that progressives devote to training candidates on the intricacies of running for office and volunteers in the manner of how to campaign should not be overlooked. Progressives in the Hudson Valley carved out an important role as civic educators, not only playing integral roles on campaigns but helping voters by ensuring that campaigns give citizens information to make informed decisions.

Progressives coordinate volunteers inside and outside the political party structure. Many employed extra-party, nonprofit means such as Indivisible, NY19 Votes, Mountain Top Progressives, and other groups to coordinate and organize electoral activism. Progressives played an integral role in the election of Antonio Delgado and a number of state senate candidates. They even organized to campaign outside of the Hudson Valley for Anthony Brindisi. These progressive activists also engaged in a number of activities through these organizations to identify voters with two homes in the state and approach these citizens about registering to vote in the Hudson Valley.

And progressives run for public office. Some run with no hope of winning but to bring light to important issues. Others develop a platform and hope to be elected but come up short once the votes are counted. Others need to run for office more than once in order to win. Some are elected their first time running. And, in several instances, progressives ran for office because they were asked to run and felt a sense of civic obligation to either help the group that asked them to be candidates, to help the residents of the political unit where they sought office, or to run to ensure that people have a choice on Election Day.

The evidence presented in this chapter illustrates that there is a robust progressive presence in the Hudson Valley. Progressives serve a sacred function, giving voters a choice at the polls. Indeed, they are a core part of making democracy work. Without them, the electoral arena in the Hudson Valley would be a less vibrant place. And they use government and nonprofits to fight the status quo in order to advance equity and equal opportunity. That is why they seek office. That is why they campaign for certain candidates.

But it is also important to note that while this chapter shows that there is a robust progressive presence in the Hudson Valley, the results have wider implications. Indeed, the work also supports the supposition that there is a robust progressive presence outside of major metropolitan areas. Indeed, progressives are active in rural, suburban, and urban areas. As such, left-wing activism is not simply a function of several boroughs of New York City—or other big cities. Progressives can be found even in places that we do not expect, like rural Greene County or semirural parts of Dutchess County. As such, the implications of this work continue to show that it matters far beyond the borders of the Hudson Valley.

This study also shows that political engagement does not begin and end on Election Day. Progressives are an essential part of the policymaking process that does not necessarily include electoral politics. We will now see how they contribute to state and local policymaking—using the government and nonprofits to fight the status quo and advance equity and equal opportunity.

Chapter 4

Progressive Activists in the Policy Arena

Progressive activists are robustly involved in the policy arena. They lobby and contact government elites, draft and adopt policies as elected and appointed officials, speak at town hall and policymaking meetings, gather petitions, hold public rallies, educate the public, build coalitions, conduct research, engage in civil disobedience, and leverage their positions in nonprofit organizations. This book is largely about state and local policy battles, and the particular federal nature of the American polity illustrates the policy decisions that take place in state houses; county seats; and village, town, and city halls fall within the realms of reserved and concurrent powers.

It should be no surprise then that progressives engage in discussions and battles in the following policy areas: environmental, parks, labor, land use, economic development, government organization, elections, and education. Additionally, while immigration is not a reserved or concurrent power, criminal justice policy surrounding enforcement of immigration falls within the realm of public safety, which is indeed in the jurisdiction of states and municipalities. Therefore, local immigration protection and sanctuary city policies are also a noticeable part of progressives' policy agendas.

Their activities fall into four different categories. First, progressives successfully help to manufacture public policy. Second, they effectively advocate for governments to not make policies that progressives believe are damaging. Third, progressives encourage particular solutions to problems but fail in their quests to have their desired policy goals adopted. Fourth, progressives attempt to stop governments from making decisions that they believe are detrimental but do not achieve their desired goals.

Figure 4.1. Progressive policy activities fall into either advocating for the adoption of policy solutions or working to stop undesired policy proposals. Progressives may or may not be successful in meeting their objectives. *Source:* Created by the author.

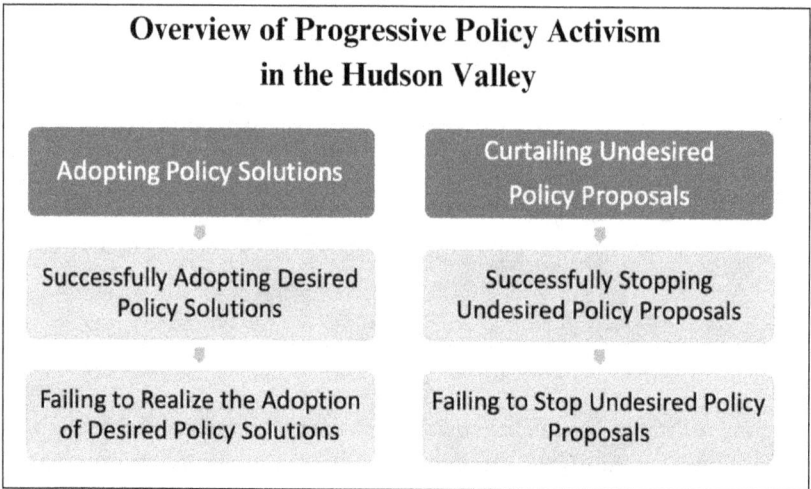

Overview of Progressive Policy Activism in the Hudson Valley

Adopting Policy Solutions	Curtailing Undesired Policy Proposals
Successfully Adopting Desired Policy Solutions	Successfully Stopping Undesired Policy Proposals
Failing to Realize the Adoption of Desired Policy Solutions	Failing to Stop Undesired Policy Proposals

The data explained in the following section illustrate that progressives cannot be ignored in the Hudson Valley policy arena. They are, indeed, a robust and visible part of the political landscape in the Hudson Valley. But their policy activism also shows, more broadly, that left-of-center political activism is found in areas outside of America's largest cities. Indeed, progressives apply their craft in urban, suburban, and rural areas. And they fight the status quo in order to advance equity and equal opportunity.

Successfully Adopting Desired Policy Solutions

Progressive political activists have an impact on the policy process. They successfully labored to adopt a number of environmental policies. This should come as no surprise as environmental activism in the Hudson Valley is particularly well known and documented (Lifset 2014; Schuyler 2018). Progressives were also successful by playing a part in realizing their preferred policy solutions in the following policy areas: land use, labor, government structure, immigration, and education. Thus, there is a robust progressive presence in the Hudson Valley's policy arena. The policy proposals that they helped implement fight the status quo in order to advance equity and equal opportunity. And they use governments and nonprofits as means of achieving these goals.

ENVIRONMENTAL

Community Choice Aggregation

Community Choice Aggregation (CCA) allows a municipality in New York, at its own discretion, to pass a local law that gives a particular gas and electricity producer preference to deliver its utilities to energy consumers in the confines of the municipality (New York State Energy Research and Development Authority 2021). Importantly, individual customers residing in the confines of a participating municipality are able to choose to not participate in the program, if they wish. Further, the requirements of the program ensure that the energy is from renewable sources, as indicated in the New York State Energy and Research Authority's Step-by-Step Guidance presentation (2021). Environmentally conscious progressive activists have been advocating for local governments to take advantage of this program.

Jason Angell of Putnam County happily told me that he worked for three years to realize a renewable electricity program that began on July 1, 2019. Angell explained that commercial and residential electricity consumers in a number of municipalities, including Philipstown, Beacon, Fishkill, Cold Spring, and the city of Poughkeepsie began receiving their electricity from renewable energy sources. Angell disclosed that over a three-year period, he advocated for municipal officials to adopt CCA ordinances in their jurisdictions. This advocacy included giving over forty presentations to these elected officials. Each community that adopted CCA now bulk purchases renewable electricity together. Angell explained that bulk purchasing electricity gives municipalities the same cost savings that major corporations receive. Clearly, local progressive activism matters.

Angell asked, "What is the most radical thing you can imagine locally? And then how do you get it done?" He reported, "I'm evolving towards becoming a radical localist. And so that's where we concentrate our energy: our local projects that can be implemented within communities that we live in or are close to." Angell recounted that the first thing on his agenda as a "radical localist" was to advocate to see CCA adopted, first in Westchester County. Importantly, local ordinances are the key to the adoption of CCA.

Angell recalled that many individuals thought the plan appeared to espouse socialist principles. He countered this claim by explaining that

Central Hudson, the energy company throughout much of the Hudson Valley, determines the electricity consumers receive, and that consumer cost savings is not their goal. Additionally, Angell told me that 80 percent of the electricity that Central Hudson uses, at the time of our interview, was not renewable. Angell also noted working with a Poughkeepsie city councilmember on the project.

Angell declared, upon the adoption of the program in 2019, roughly seventy thousand individuals in the municipalities that adopted CCA transitioned to cheaper, renewable energy. Clearly, Angell's progressive presence mattered in advocating for local laws to purchase renewable energy.

Angell noted that activists started working on the project at the end of 2015. It took four years of laboring to achieve this policy goal. Angell observed, "So, to me that's like radical localism. You just made the automatic electricity supplier for seventy thousand people. I think it was thirty-five thousand electricity accounts, 100 percent renewable energy. For people that care . . . they're psyched. For people who don't care at all, they're just never going to notice any difference." As of this writing, the number of Hudson Valley municipalities that participate in the program has grown to a total of ten (Joule Community Power 2021). Per the homepage for the program, in the intervening period between its launch in July of 2019 and the time of this writing, "220,000 metric tons of greenhouse gas emissions have been avoided" due to buy-in from the ten municipalities participating.

Angell proudly stated that activists do not need to only believe that reforms can occur in state or national policy arenas, but there are opportunities locally as well, particularly if activists are creative. CCA was clearly a policy success, and the adoption of local laws was certainly assisted by progressive activists like Jason Angell, who was elected to the Philipstown Town Board in 2021.

Climate Smart Certification

In January of 2019, the Tuxedo Town Board passed the Climate Smart Community Task Force Pledge (Town of Tuxedo 2019). This started the process of the town becoming certified as a Climate Smart Community, which indicates that they went through a formal assessment to ensure the town met a series of requirements that would ameliorate climate change issues (Climate Smart Communities n.d.). Climate Smart Community certification brings with it both environmental and economic benefits.

Dr. Maria May, who was elected to the Tuxedo Town Board in 2019, told me that this includes changing the energy source in the town to renewable energy. She informed me that the town was in the process of receiving Climate Smart Certification that will save people roughly 15 percent of their energy costs. Dr. May continued, recalling that the opponents to the plan were bothered that the entire community would be automatically signed up to participate in the plan. But, Dr. May noted, anyone can choose to not participate. She expressed that an opponent of the certification argued that it should not be up to him to tell people which energy supplier they should use. But Dr. May replied that the company helping people save energy costs sends all customers a form to opt out of the program. She argued that it was not the town deciding, and that 15 percent is a great deal of money for those having trouble heating their houses during a Hudson Valley winter.

Dr. May reported that Climate Smart Certification requires that town vehicles must be electric and town electricity be solar powered. She noted that the cost of renewable energy saves money in the long run, after an initial outlay of cash. Further, she explained that New York State gives municipalities grants to help cover the cost of transition. Thus, this certification process seems to be an important victory for progressives as they work for a cleaner environment.

Coeymans Clean Air Legislation

In March of 2019, the town of Coeymans located at the southern tip of Albany County adopted the Coeymans Clean Air Law (Willard 2019). Christine Primomo of Albany County highlighted this law in her discussion of progressive policy successes. The local law came about in response to a local cement plant's plan to burn trash as a source of energy in the village of Ravena, which is located in the town of Coeymans (Willard 2019; Hallisay 2020). Christine Primomo observed that the ordinance would curtail any business in Coeymans from disposing of garbage in incinerators or in the smokestack of the cement plant. The cement plant is a major employer in the area (Willard 2019). Local progressives worked diligently with the Coeymans Town Board to have this local law adopted.

Primomo noted that out of the five-member town board, three Democrats supported the measure and two Republicans opposed the ordinance. She also extolled that the law is novel, being the first of its type in the nation. Primomo recounted the story behind her involvement. She explained, in December of 2017, another Hudson Valley activist received a correspondence from the Energy Justice Network in Pennsylvania, who was working on another incinerator campaign in a different state. Primomo reported that the Energy Justice Network discovered that a Connecticut-based company proposed to move trash from Connecticut to the cement plant located in Coeymans to use as fuel in their incinerators. Upon receiving this information, this activist began organizing.

Primomo revealed that the activist received this information a few days before Christmas, and they worked together to organize a news conference, which was well attended by concerned citizens and the media. Primomo recalled that as a result of this, town officials hired an attorney to craft a clean air ordinance that "would limit to very specific amounts, any kind of incinerated fuels that are trucked in from anywhere to certain amounts a day . . . it didn't forbid it, but it did restrict and put guidelines." The law limited the amount of waste a company can burn in the town to twenty-five tons per day (Willard 2019).

The local company was vehemently opposed to the ordinance. Primomo remembered that the ordinance took a great deal of time to pass and that the board kept rescheduling the vote. She explained that in support of the effort, activists began a postcard campaign, where they sent postcards to five hundred town residents educating them about the issue. Christine told me that she worked with two other activists who largely spearheaded the effort. Primomo recalled that an activist she knows was involved with a prominent advocacy group in the county and this activist sent information about the news conference to many individuals they each knew. Christine observed that the issue is not simply a matter for Coeymans as the by-product of burning the trash disperses into a shared atmosphere. In addition to postcards, activists also wrote letters and made phone calls to town board members and sent newspapers letters to the editor. Primomo also noted that they had two postcard parties where they lobbied the Albany County Legislature to pass a similar ordinance.

After the town board passed the ordinance, town Republicans ran against the town supervisor and the two incumbent Democratic town board members. Primomo described the GOP plan as "a full court press" to defeat the Democrats and repeal the ordinance. Indeed, on December 2, 2020, the Coeymans Town Board, without a dissenting vote, passed amendments to the ordinance that "declaws" the law, after Republicans took control of the body (Hallisay 2020).

It is undeniable that progressive activists worked to narrowly pass clean air legislation and were successful at doing so. In that sense, they realized a policy victory. That said, the victory was ephemeral. New power dynamics led to the repeal of the town ordinance. But that is not the entire story.

Albany County Executive Dan McCoy signed into law the Albany County Clean Air Act in September of 2020 that "bans industrial waste burning within the county and prohibits opening new waste incinerators. The ban includes the burning of aqueous film-forming foam at the Norlite facility in Cohoes and tire burning at the LafargeHolcim Cement Plant in Ravena" (Fego 2020). As such, progressives in the Capital District clearly had an impact on public policy, perhaps ephemerally in the town of Coeymans, but far more lasting in Albany County as a whole.

Pilgrim Pipeline

Pilgrim Pipeline, LLC—for whom the Pilgrim Pipeline is named—proposed the construction of a conduit to carry Bakken crude oil from Albany, New York, to Linden, New Jersey. The pipe would stretch the entire length of the Hudson Valley (Sierra Club New Jersey Chapter n.d.). Per the Sierra Club and the Coalition Against Pilgrim Pipeline, fracking would be employed to extract Bakken crude oil, which the Sierra Club reported is "the most explosive."

Given the history of environmental activism in the Hudson Valley, it should come as no surprise that progressive activists campaigned against constructing the proposed pipeline. Dr. Maria May of Orange County disclosed that the proposed pipeline would run directly through Tuxedo Park, which sparked legal maneuvering to create a consolidated "village town village," which Dr. May reported is the first of its kind in New York. More precisely, the voters created a second village in the confines of the town in order to ensure that every square inch of the town is represented by a village government. Dr. May explained that towns are not granted the powers to regulate pipelines to the degree that villages can, and as such, the town voted to create a second village that is completely within the town of Tuxedo. As such, there will be two villages in the town of Tuxedo—one that is coterminous with the entire town. The vote on the creation of the village was 478 to 23 (McKenna 2019). Tuxedo was not the only municipality engaged in efforts to thwart the pipeline.

Lin Sakai discovered information about the proposed pipeline very early in the planning process. She recalled how quickly activists organized and began canvassing door to door in Plattekill in opposition to the pipeline. Sakai told me about efforts to simply inform homeowners about the proposal to construct a pipeline through their town. Sakai noted that activists started attending town board meetings and campaigned to have town boards pass resolutions expressing opposition to the Pilgrim Pipeline. Sakai mentioned that opposition to the pipeline crossed party lines. Town boards controlled by both Democrats and Republicans passed nonbinding resolutions declaring their opposition to the project.

Sakai recalled the widespread efforts of local activists who took up the mantle of going door to door to educate residents about the proposal. And she noted that the Ulster County Legislature also passed a resolution voicing opposition to the Pilgrim Pipeline by a vote of 22 to 1 (Ulster County Legislature 2015). Over thirty municipalities, including Ulster County and the New Paltz Central School District, passed resolutions opposing construction of the pipeline (Coalition Against Pilgrim Pipeline n.d.a). Sakai noted, "And then, nothing happened. It's like they stopped." She affirmed that efforts to construct the pipeline were abandoned.

The effort to stop the Pilgrim Pipeline resulted in the passage of over thirty municipal resolutions voicing opposition to the project's construction. And residents of Tuxedo voted to form a new local government entity in their quest to foil the proposal. First, it is clear that this was not a progressive victory alone, but that progressives were a key part of the coalition of like-minded individuals opposing the pipeline. Second, while the municipal resolutions opposing the conduit were not the silver bullet curtailing the project, they nevertheless were a policy tool used to engage the public. And, at the very least, these efforts illustrate that there is a robust progressive presence in the Hudson Valley, and progressives used government and nonprofit policy tools that they had at their disposal to seek a desired outcome to a policy problem. Beyond this, there is clearly a progressive presence in rural, suburban, and urban areas outside of America's largest cities. Finally, environmental equity is, indeed, a form of equity. And, here too, progressives fought diligently for equity.

Solid Waste Facility Moratorium

A company proposed constructing a facility in Rensselaer County that would turn municipal waste into fuel that might be burned in facilities including, but not limited to, cement plants (Karlin 2019). Christine Primomo explained that activists organized a group opposing the project in Rensselaer

County and garnered the support of Republicans on the county legislature. An ordinance passed that "prohibits, for a period of one (1) year from the effective date of this Local Law, the approval, permitting or opening of any solid waste management facility, including, but not limited to, landfills and transfer stations, in Rensselaer County within a one (1) mile distance from the Hudson River" (Rensselaer County Legislature 2019). Further, in September, the legislature expanded the moratorium on the "expansion of, or opening of any Solid Waste Management Facility" within one mile of the Hudson River or the source of any municipal water supply (Rensselaer County Legislature 2019).

Primomo reported that the legislature and progressive activists want to guarantee that commercial enterprises being established in Rensselaer County and the city of Rensselaer continue to prevent the area from becoming a dumping ground. Progressives were not the only reason that these moratoriums occurred. But they were a part of a coalition that convinced a Republican-controlled legislature to pass two ordinances without a single vote against each proposal.

Parks

Jen Fuentes of Ulster County told me of her time working for the city of Kingston. She stated, "I'm a very good-government type of person. So, even if I don't necessarily agree, I'm going to play by the rules that are laid out." Fuentes, concerning her administration of federal money from the Department of Housing and Urban Development, noted that she, with the support of a former mayor, changed the focus of the money to help those with lower and modest incomes. Fuentes explained that she focused on moving money into Midtown Kingston, an area that has typically been overlooked.

Fuentes is extremely proud of the razing of a debilitated motel on Broadway that was called the King's Inn. I personally spent much time driving on Broadway over a number of years, and I can attest to the eyesore that was the King's Inn. I clearly remember that there was a broken window with a pillow shoved into the opening where glass should have been. The pillow was in that space for years.

Fuentes oversaw the demolition of the King's Inn and the construction of a parking area and a "green space" where people from the community were able to come together. Fuentes also told me that she was able to see a small park built on a public housing site, which she noted was contentious as she aimed to install a place where people can play basketball.

Jen Fuentes was not the only progressive involved in parks. Ginny O'Brien of Rensselaer County explained that she became engaged in issues surrounding town parks because of poorly maintained equipment and anemic park programs. O'Brien then brought different stakeholders together through the creation of a Parks Taskforce. Members included staff in the town building department and various members of the community who were vested in maintaining and highlighting town parks. O'Brien told me about a park festival that these activists organized that included merchants and amusement rides for children. This event led to new equipment being purchased that greatly enhanced the parks. O'Brien engaged in other activities on the town board to help with the creation, improvement, and maintenance of parks.

O'Brien highlighted a grant that was written during her tenure as a town board member that constructed a new park in a residential part of the town. Many people walked to this park. And a bocce court was built, and concerts were held. O'Brien noted the park clearly illustrated to residents how taxes were being used. She expressed, "The complaint I heard all the time was where do our taxes go? We pay so much; we don't see anything." O'Brien said her work with local parks made residents feel affinity toward their community.

The work that Jen Fuentes and Ginny O'Brien did on parks clearly illustrates that progressives are a robust part of the Hudson Valley policymaking community and play a role in policy successes throughout the region. Further, the work clearly illustrates that progressives do not simply exist in America's largest cities. And these policy successes helped achieve equity, particularly in the case of Midtown Kingston, which had been ignored and underfunded for years.

Assessment of Environmental Work

Progressives successfully engaged in a number of environmental policy battles. Importantly, in most instances, they were parts of coalitions that worked to adopt policy solutions. Progressives were not the only reason why these desired policies were adopted. But progressives appear to be a key part of either a formal or informal coalition, an administration, or a legislative body that advances an agenda where environmental concerns are prominently featured and considered.

The aforementioned stories illustrate that progressives used government to adopt policies and nonprofit means to fight for policies. Further, in each of these instances, progressives were battling against the status quo. I also believe that these victories brought about equity and equal opportunity for several reasons. First, some communities have clean environments, and some do not. Progressives sought to provide equity in terms of pushing for a cleaner, greener environment. Second, indeed, environmental problems come with a host of issues that prevent opportunity for large portions of the population. Environmentally induced health issues or diminished economic or educational prospects due to environmental concerns diminish both equity and equal opportunity.

But also, these stories reveal that progressives were active in the Hudson Valley and were found in areas outside of the biggest cities in the United States. Indeed, they were found in rural, suburban, and urban areas of the region. Beyond the environment, progressives also successfully engaged in policy battles in other realms.

LAND USE AND ECONOMIC DEVELOPMENT

John Gromada of Rockland County was deeply concerned about housing affordability in his village. In order to help adapt desired policy solutions to the housing crisis, he worked with his wife to adopt affordable housing requirements in Nyack. He noted that his wife, who served as a village trustee, was able to see the adoption of a requirement that 20 percent of new housing construction would be affordable. He asserted that this was a policy success. However, Gromada lamented that the village government either cutback the requirement or gave developers a way to bypass these regulations. As such, this progressive policy success in Nyack came about through progressive efforts, even if it was short-lived.

The city of Hudson is also heavily involved in land use and economic development issues. In particular, Kamal Johnson, elected mayor of Hudson following our interview, divulged that the local birthing center in the city moved to Albany, due to a drop in existing population as the city becomes gentrified. He argued that this has an impact on families and curbs interest in moving to Hudson permanently. Johnson explained that much of this population loss is due to the proliferation of short-term rental properties.

Johnson asserted that there is a severe housing shortage due to the city hosting over three hundred short-term rental units. That is in a city of just under six thousand residents, per Johnson. Following his election as mayor in 2019, Johnson signed an ordinance regulating short-term rentals (Schneider 2020). Schneider tells readers that the local law does not ban short-term rentals. The policy, which passed the Hudson Common Council unanimously, allows for up to three short-term rental units as long as a resident of the city operates these units on the same property where the resident resides. The president of the Hudson Common Council, Tom DePietro, asserted that the law was adopted to "preserve community character and make Hudson a place that people want to visit and live in . . . To visit and live in" (Schneider 2020). Kamal Johnson and Hudson progressives also had other plans for land use and economic development.

Mayor Johnson told me he was working on legislation to adopt inclusionary zoning. Johnson explained that this type of zoning mandates a particular number of affordable housing units. He also told me about a local nonprofit that owns roughly eighty parcels of land in the city that are not being developed. As such, he has been lobbying this foundation to develop those properties into housing units. Further, in September of 2021, Johnson signed a good cause eviction law that mandates landlords must have a "good cause" to not renew a tenant's lease (Hannigan Gilson 2021). Hannigan Gilson reported that the ordinance passed with just a single abstention. Clearly, progressives in the city of Hudson enjoyed a number of policy successes.

Pat Strong of Ulster County told me of another progressive policy success. Strong reported that city of Kingston Mayor Steve Noble worked to create the Kingston City Land Bank. Strong told me through this entity, foreclosed properties are renovated and then are sold to buyers who have low or moderate incomes. Strong observed that this vehicle "is a much more equitable way to dispose of foreclosed properties." This is meant to curtail developers from procuring these properties for very low prices. Strong was involved in this effort; she has a robust background in nonprofits. The organization of the landbank is fascinating.

Under state law, the city of Kingston established a land bank as a 501(c) 3 charitable organization, whose board of directors consists of nine directors appointed by the mayor of Kingston (Kingston City Landbank 2024). The landbank's bylaws also state that under the New York Public Authorities Accountability Act of 2005, the directors will have the powers of "boards of public benefit corporations and local public authorities." The landbank purchased its first three properties in July of 2020 (City of Kingston 2020). The city of Kingston explained that as properties are refurbished, they will largely be sold to households "earning at or below 100 percent of the Area Median Income in Ulster County." At the time of this writing, this is $83,700 gross, for a family of four; and there is an open application to purchase the property (City of Kingston 2020). The press release also noted that the Kingston City Landbank's mission "is to foster an equitable community where vacant or distressed properties are transformed into community assets that improve the quality of life for Kingston residents, stabilize and enhance neighborhoods, and create new pathways for social and economic development." Thus, the city of Kingston, through the efforts of local progressives inside and outside of government, enjoyed a significant policy success.

This section on land use and economic development clearly illustrates that progressives have a robust presence in the Hudson Valley and in areas outside of America's major cities. Further, progressives are a visible and important part of the policymaking arena throughout the region. And progressives use governments and nonprofit entities to fight the status quo in the hope of advancing equity and equal opportunity.

LABOR

Working Families Party state committee member David Schwartz was actively involved in two efforts to raise the wages of workers. The first victory came about in November of 2002 and affected Westchester County.

David Schwartz spent a great deal of time working for Westchester County to enact a living wage ordinance, particularly one geared at home healthcare and other service workers whose employers enter into service contracts with Westchester County. He told me of the details of the policy campaign that he largely managed. Through this campaign, he assembled a coalition to lobby the county. He noted the assistance of George Latimer, who at the time of this policy question chaired the Westchester County Board of Legislators. Schwartz recounted that while it did not achieve everything the campaign wanted, it did give home healthcare workers and several building service employees a living wage. He reflected, "When I look back now when people are talking a $15 minimum wage fourteen years later, we got $13.50 an hour, as long as it included $1.50 an hour for health benefits." Schwartz proclaimed, "And we won that." Indeed, in November of 2002, the Westchester County Board of Legislators passed Schwartz's proposal into law by a vote of 12 to 3 (Brennen Center for Justice 2002). Schwartz's next effort was geared at statewide policy.

David Schwartz and the Working Families Party leveraged fusion voting laws in their journey to pass a higher state minimum wage. The story goes back to the 2004 election cycle. Schwartz recalled that the state assembly would vote to increase the state minimum wage every year, and then the bill would never be addressed by the state senate, which had a Republican majority. David recalled that then New York State Senator Nick Spano, who represented part of Westchester County, was a senior member of the body who found himself in a district with shifting demographics. David Schwartz recalled that Spano was a member of the Republican majority in the senate but, due to these demographic changes, knew that his partisan affiliation was going to make it hard for him to be reelected. As such, per Schwartz, Senator Spano would have been greatly aided by the endorsement of the Working Families Party. So, David, the vice chair of the Westchester-Putnam Chapter of the Working Families Party, met with Senator Spano.

At the meeting Schwartz told Senator Spano to increase the minimum wage by $2.10 per hour. Senator Spano told the Working Families Party that he would do his best. In response, local progressive activists told him, in the words of David Schwartz, "You don't try. You do it. You're the third ranking" member of the senate. They also informed Spano that they want him to secure enough votes to override a potential gubernatorial veto.

David Schwartz then recounted his group's plan of action following this meeting. They knocked on doors in parts of Senator Spano's district that were marginal. They brought with them blank paper, writing instruments, and clipboards. And they asked residents to compose handwritten notes to Senator Spano to ask him to vote to increase the minimum wage. Their goal was ten notes per canvasser each day they were going door to door. David Schwartz remembered, "I would stand in the doorway. Some of these people wouldn't have shoes and socks on and it was freezing cold, and so many wrote." David Schwartz then noted that they held a public rally in Yonkers where between sixty and seventy people showed up to support the minimum wage increase. Schwartz recalled that Senator Spano signed a poster-sized pledge to support the increase. Schwartz told me that the Working Families Party gave Spano, a Republican, its line in the general election, instead of giving their line to Andrea Stewart-Cousins in her first campaign for the seat in 2004. Schwartz emphasized that eight hundred citizens cast ballots on the Working Families Party line in that election, and Spano won the race against Stewart-Cousins by just eighteen votes (New York State Board of Elections 2004).

David Schwartz told us that there was great anger directed at the Working Families Party for giving its line to Spano over a progressive candidate like Stewart-Cousins. Schwartz affirmed, "I certainly had no problem saying to people, three quarters of a million New Yorkers got a $2.10 increase . . . It was worth doing. That's what this party is all about. She wasn't going to get it as the junior senator, no matter how progressive. And anyway, they get elected every two years. So, two years later she walloped him with our support." Indeed, this was another progressive policy success.

Progressive activist David Schwartz, with the support of like-minded progressives in and out of the party structure, was heavily involved in two successful efforts to raise the pay of various employees. These stories continue to demonstrate that there is a robust progressive presence in the Hudson Valley and in areas outside of America's largest cities, and that these activists are an important part of the policy process. Further, the stories clearly show that activists used government and nonprofit organizations to fight for equity and equal opportunity.

GOVERNMENT STRUCTURES

John Schwartz of Ulster County described the creation of the office of Ulster County Executive. He told me that the referendum to create the office was contentious. John Schwartz recounted a number of policy successes and achievements since the office's creation, including the rail trail network that created a mechanism for bikers to ride from the Poughkeepsie Train Station, to a number of parts of Ulster County, to the Catskills. John Schwartz asserted that the creation of this, and other attractions, can be linked to the Ulster County Executive's office, who is able to act as a centralized point to plan short-term and long-term goals for the county. Previously, there was no county executive, and a member of the county legislature, elected from one district in the county, served as chair of the body. But that legislative chair did not have buy-in from the entire county—a county executive does. As such, more organization is possible with a county executive. He called this a policy success.

John Schwartz affirmed that there was opposition to the creation of the position. He noted that it was widely believed that Democrat Mike Hein would win the position without much competition. Indeed, Hein held the post from 2009 to the beginning of 2019. John Schwartz explained that Republicans simply did not want to give Hein power; they were not really opposed to the creation of the position. The new charter that created the office was passed by voters at the 2006 General Election with 20,149 votes in favor and 18,785 votes against (Ulster County Board of Elections 2006). Ulster County also had a battle over term limits for county officials.

Andrew Zink told me that term limits were a key part of his platform in his campaign for county legislator and noted that just prior to our conversation, a term limit bill was signed into office by Ulster County Executive Pat Ryan. The term limit legislation restricts the Ulster County Executive, the Ulster County Comptroller, and Ulster County Legislators to no more than twelve years in office in each position (Ulster County 2019). Ryan noted, "In passing and signing this law we are recognizing that we have to constantly reinvigorate our democracy . . . No elected office should ever belong to an individual, it must always remain in the hands of the people" (Ulster County 2019). Thus, this came about with bipartisan support. And not all progressives support term limits. But it is important to note that some progressives were a part of the coalition that brought a constitutionally sound form of term limits into effect in Ulster County.

First, it is clear that there is a robust progressive presence in the Hudson Valley and in rural, suburban, and urban areas outside of America's biggest cities. Second, these are instances where progressives used government to fight the status quo. It is also clear, certainly in the case of the fight for term limits, that the battle was to achieve equity and equal opportunity in order to make arrangements for candidates for public office to not run against incumbents, and, therefore, increase their likelihood of electoral success in open seats. Concerning the creation of a county executive, the position broke down disjointed power arrangements and created an office that had electoral accountability to the entire county. Before this post was established, the chair of the county legislature would steer policy. This legislator was chosen by other legislators, not voters, to be chair of the body. And, as legislators are elected from districts, this chair only had an electoral relationship with the voters of just one legislative district. The creation of the position of Ulster County Executive helped to bring about equity and equal opportunity for voters to choose their county's chief executive. And that was created through government policy.

Sanctuary Movement, Welcoming and Inclusive Municipalities, and Local Law Enforcement

Large numbers of progressives mobilized to assist the immigrant community. These activists were horrified by the rhetoric and the policies coming from the Trump administration on this issue. Progressives advocated for municipalities to adopt sanctuary or "welcoming and inclusive" designations.

Pat Strong told me that during Kingston Mayor Steve Noble's administration, the city of Kingston designated itself as welcoming and inclusive. Strong noted that it is not a synonym for *sanctuary city*, and there are distinctions between the terms, but the two terms are on the same spectrum. Indeed, the Kingston Common Council passed a resolution on a 5 to 3 vote "declaring the city 'welcoming and inclusive' toward undocumented immigrants, who won't be asked for paperwork during first encounters with police" (Kemble 2017). Kingston was not the only city to declare itself welcoming and inclusive.

Connie Hogarth of Dutchess County recalled Beacon's process of becoming welcoming and inclusive. She told me that adopting this designation was difficult because while the council was controlled by the Democratic Party, the mayor was not a Democrat. She also noted that while the city did not designate itself as a sanctuary city, they do not cooperate with ICE and are functionally a sanctuary city, even if they did not adopt the formal title. *The Highlands Current* reported, "On April 3, the Beacon City Council unanimously passed a similar resolution declaring the city to be 'welcoming, safe and inclusive' but also avoiding sanctuary" (Schevtchuk Armstrong 2017). Hogarth noted that the city of Newburgh, in Orange County too, even though it has many more African American and Latino residents, did not adopt the term *sanctuary city* but, in practice, implemented the policies associated with that term. Other localities adopted similar policies.

Philipstown in Putnam County followed the pattern (Schevtchuk Armstrong 2017). *The Highlands Current* chronicled the passage of the local law to guarantee "equal protection" to town residents, irrespective of their naturalization classification, and prohibited Philipstown staff from cooperating with federal immigration officers. Andrew Falk of Putnam County also highlighted that Philipstown passed a sanctuary ordinance in our conversations.

One of the progressive activists who contributed time to this study was also featured in the story by *The Highlands Current*. Schevtchuk Armstrong wrote, "Jason Angell said that residents should not conflate terrorism with the question of undocumented immigrants. 'It's not about stopping ISIS [with] local law enforcement,' he said." Further, the article notes that Angell gave a history of undocumented immigrants, asserting that undocumented immigration was encouraged as a means of providing a cheap labor force, but today, corporations find it even more cost effective to outsource their plants to other nations (Schevtchuk Armstrong 2017). And more municipalities adopted similar policies.

Maria Quackenbush recalled that the Dutchess County Progressive Action Alliance worked to have the Poughkeepsie Common Council designate the city as a sanctuary city. Barry reported that the city of Poughkeepsie, at the time of declaring itself a "Safe City," a term designated by the Department of Law under Attorney General Schneiderman, was already not cooperating with federal immigration officials (2017). Nevertheless, the city adopted the designation formally. Per Barry, the vote was unanimous. Again, the city of Poughkeepsie officially used other language than sanctuary city but captured the spirit of the movement.

Kamal Johnson told me that the city of Hudson adopted a sanctuary policy in 2017. He recalled that there was minor resistance but noted that most residents supported the policy. WAMC reported that the Hudson City Council adopted a "Resolution Affirming Hudson as a Welcoming and Inclusive City" by a vote of 10 to 1 (Dunne 2017). Dunne (2017) noted that the resolution was based on the state attorney general's guidelines.

Supervisor Linda Mussmann, who also lives in the city of Hudson, observed, "I think the sanctuary movement in Columbia County has been a very powerful force. There's been a huge amount of organizing around . . . making sure ICE doesn't take people away." Supervisor Mussmann observed that this is a prominent social justice issue that rallied many activists hoping to protect local Hispanic residents. County government was also involved in passing immigrant protection ordinances.

A number of the contributors to this work identified the Westchester Immigrant Protection Act as a policy success. Dr. Charles Chesnavage noted that the Westchester Board of Legislators tried to pass a local law while Rob Astorino was county executive, but Astorino vetoed the measure. Chesnavage observed that the policy was adopted when Rob Astorino lost reelection. Kat Brezler noted that the policy, that is very local in nature, seems like a policy success. Mark Lieberman reported that under the ordinance, county law enforcement does not cooperate with federal immigration officials unless they are legally required to do so. Tasha Young observed that the policy was "preemptive" based on the Trump administration's rhetoric but considered the law a success. Young recalled that the law prevents municipalities from working with Immigration and Customs Enforcement, and she believes the law was "a progressive win."

Nada Khader explained the situation in detail. She clarified that the Immigrant Protection Act mandates that county law enforcement will not furnish ICE with data unless required under law; the ordinance also had a legal impact on jails in Westchester. Prior to the signing of this law, Khader told me about a number of local raids by ICE that greatly scared residents. She noted that parents "don't send their children to school when they hear of an ICE raid. It's just extremely disruptive, extremely traumatic." Khader told me that the Mamaroneck Police Department publicly stated that no one should open their doors for anyone claiming to be an immigration enforcement official without first calling the Mamaroneck Police to make sure that the agent has a warrant. Khader asserted that she believed this statement was a way of the department showing that they stand with residents and also do not care for raids by immigration officials. Khader recalled that several local police chiefs directed all personnel to not inquire about immigration status. Khader reported that this question has been particularly prominent in the county jail, which is home to an ICE office, where people brought in must answer a question about their nation of birth.

Finally, Khader noted that the police chief in White Plains declared that a local undocumented person helping police to solve a crime will be provided with a path to a US visa, which would make their presence in the United States legal. When I asked Nada Khader if these are policy successes, she responded, "Yes. Oh, definitely." That said, some local executives took unitary action to protect immigrants from local law enforcement.

Kathy Sheehan, the mayor of the city of Albany, issued an executive order "Regarding Community Policing and Protection of Immigrants" in 2017 (Lucas 2017). *Esther Dodson* explained that while she was happy that the mayor issued an executive order on the matter, they still want the city council to pass a resolution since it is more stable than an executive order. Just across the river from Albany, Rensselaer County is the "only county in New York State to participate in ICE's 287(g) program, which deputizes local law enforcement to act as federal immigration officers" (New York Immigrant Coalition 2018). *Dodson* observed that it is interesting that these two counties are next to each other. *Dodson* also noted that Mayor Sheehan's actions show that the city is indeed a sanctuary city and has worked to exemplify that designation. *Dodson* called Sheehan's actions progressive. *Esther Dodson* told me, "The idea that all people are created equal and if they live here, they deserve the same benefits as anybody else. And so that in a way has driven the county to be more progressive."

Lucas (2017) reported the executive order forbids city employees from asking for documentation about citizenship. Lucas wrote that Sheehan stated the executive order "ensures residents will be treated with equity and will have access to services regardless of immigration status." The article quoted Albany Mayor Kathy Sheehan explaining that residents calling to report a crime should not be concerned about someone inquiring about their immigration designation (Lucas 2017).

Progressives worked with municipal officials to adopt policies that declare themselves either safe or welcoming and inclusive. This was done by ordinance in most cases, but also by executive order in the city of Albany. Indeed, progressives are a robust part of the policymaking arena in the Hudson Valley and realized important policy victories in each subregion of the Hudson Valley. These tales also illustrate that progressives are not simply found in America's largest cities—but in smaller urban jurisdictions, as well as in rural and suburban areas. They also used the government and nonprofit sectors to fight for equity and equal opportunity.

EDUCATION AND BAN THE BOX

Dr. Gregory Julian of Rockland County told me about his time as a school board member. He served for six years, which included one year as vice president and four years as the president. He noted the following during his tenure: "It was also a time where I was able to test the limits of how much democracy we can institute." He said that the district was divided between Haverstraw on one side and Stony Point on the other. The Haverstraw side was heavily Hispanic, while the Stony Point side of the district had a white majority. He also noted that this racial division was very much on the minds of people in the district. Dr. Julian recounted that following his election as president of the school board, he inquired if it was possible to change the bussing scheme for those in the fifth grade and above. Dr. Julian asked the school transportation company to send their buses east to west, rather than north to south. Dr. Julian explained, "So, on a very quiet level, we redrew the maps of where students attended schools. And we integrated the schools starting at the fifth grade." He noted that elementary schools were still based on neighborhoods but was proud of this integration of the older students. That was not the only impact that progressives had on local education policy.

Tasha Young, in collaboration with others, "worked on programs to end the school to prison pipeline." She noted, "In Yonkers, we worked with a coalition of people that wanted to lessen the punitive nature of school discipline and make it more restorative." Young explained that this would be achieved by increasing the number of social workers and other professionals in the mental health field to make the process of bringing students back into the community in a way that renews them, rather than castigating them through anachronistic disciplinary practices. Young recounted that through a partnership, this group began educating Yonkers teachers in how to realize this goal. Young explained that students in the district are mostly black and Hispanic. Young observed that black Americans are generally progressives because they continuously advocate for changes to systemic and institutional racism that are pervasive throughout our polity. As such, progressives had an impact on public schools and their students. In particular, there was certainly a racial justice component to these policy victories.

Progressives were also active in equity issues in higher education. Dolores Baldasare of Rockland County gleamed while telling me about her advocacy to the SUNY Board of Trustees. She recounted that she and others from the Rockland Coalition to End the New Jim Crow spoke at a State University of New York Board of Trustees meeting to support banning a question on SUNY applications asking those applying to indicate if they are felons. Baldasare recounted that this question was already removed by City University of New York Trustees on CUNY applications. Jaschik (2016) reported that the SUNY Board of Trustees voted 8 to 2 to remove this question from their applications; Baldasare told me that this process took several years. Thus, here, too, there was an equity component that progressive activists fought for and enjoyed seeing become policy.

Terence Miller informed me that Westchester County adopted Ban the Box countywide in 2018. Lungariello (2018) reported that employers in the county will no longer be able to have a question about criminal convictions on job applications. Lungariello also noted that the bill passed the Westchester Board of Legislators by an 11 to 5 vote. Westchester County Executive George Latimer signed the ordinance. And Lungariello noted that Yonkers and New Rochelle in Westchester already enacted similar laws. Thus, Ban the Box was of interest for progressives both in higher education and employment more generally.

Importantly, all of these stories illustrate that progressive activists use nonprofits to organize and lobby government to make policy that fights the status quo in support of equity and equal opportunity. Further, they show that there is a robust progressive presence in the Hudson Valley. Finally, this work continues to reveal that progressives do not simply exist in America's largest cities but in smaller urban areas, as well as rural and suburban communities.

ASSESSMENT OF SUCCESSFUL POLICY CAMPAIGNS

Progressives have been involved in victories on a cluster of issues. Their wins and support clearly illustrate their influence as actors in the policymaking process. In some instances, progressives were able to make change as elected or appointed officials. This is clearly illustrated by Kamal Johnson, Dr. Gregory Julian, and Ginny O'Brien, who used their elected positions to advance policy goals. Jen Fuentes also used her appointed policy position to bring about change. David Schwartz was able to leverage his role as a Working Families Party state committee member to see desired policy solutions come to fruition. And many others were a part of broad coalitions that usually included nonprofits, such as WESPAC.

And in many other instances, the exact impact of progressives might be less clear. That said, Christine Primomo's role in Coeymans is crystal clear; she was one of the core members of that clean air effort. Progressives were also part of a number of coalitions that might have included adherents to other political ideologies. Concerning the latter, the opposition to the Pilgrim Pipeline, the adoption of term limits in Ulster County, and the one-year solid waste moratorium in Rensselaer County were prominent bipartisan efforts.

Unquestionably, progressives were a robust part of the policymaking arena in the Hudson Valley. And their presence shows that progressives are not simply found in America's largest cities—but rural and suburban areas—as well as smaller urban communities. Sometimes they were the main drivers of policy solutions; at other times they were part of a large coalition. Importantly, they used government and nonprofit means to fight the status quo in support of policy proposals that they believe will usher in equity and equal opportunity. Progressives flexed their muscles by not only working to have desired policies approved but also by working to curtail others they saw as damaging.

Policy Proposals Successfully Stopped

All of the policy proposals that progressives were successful at curtailing were related to the environment. Given the history of environmentalism in the area, as already highlighted in this chapter, this should come as no surprise. Progressives use nonprofit organizations and government to fight the status quo of corporate attempts to construct environmentally damaging projects throughout the Hudson Valley. In doing so, they fight for environmental equity and equal opportunity to prevent Hudson Valley residents from experiencing the damaging impact of for-profit corporations.

Hudson Cement Plant

Progressives mobilized to defeat a plan to build a cement plant near the city of Hudson. *Bart Sooter* explained that cement plant opponents formed a nonprofit called Friends of Hudson that had a membership of roughly four thousand individuals and was able to raise $2.5 million to fight the plant. *Sooter* said the battle lasted seven years.

Sooter's account of the policy battle was extraordinarily detailed. He began telling me that in 1998 he received "this cheerful little postcard" from the cement company that said "'we'd like to be your new neighbor.' And my reaction was oh, shit. Because I knew what the cement industry was like, having lived in the Hudson Valley for thirty-five years." *Sooter* asserted that in the Hudson Valley, cement facilities are often owned by corporations in Europe, who treat the United States like a dumping ground. *Sooter* explained that the company proposed to construct a plant with a smokestack that would have been six hundred feet tall, and a quarry on the Hudson, making the plant one of the world's largest. Advocates opposing the plant were deeply concerned about blasting in the quarry, and dangerous and significant air pollution from the smokestack. *Sooter* further explained that the plant would impact the Hudson River, where the company proposed loading cement for transport. Further, *Sooter* argued that the company did not have a sterling reputation.

Sooter used LexisNexis to conduct research on the company. He lamented, "What I was finding was horrifying." Through his research, *Sooter* told me that he found the company had a history of being engaged in legal battles and amassing fines by environmental regulators. He explained that residents from Columbia County organized and raised $2.5 million over a seven-year period that they used to employ excellent engineers and attorneys. This prepared Friends of Hudson well for hearings on the plant. *Sooter* noted how rare it is for opponents of these large-scale projects to have the resources that Friends of Hudson enjoyed.

Sooter recounted that the group's first meeting consisted of residents sitting in a living room and planning how they were going to fight the plant. This led to the beginnings of forming a nonprofit, working with the Open Space Institute, which served as an "umbrella organization" and relieved them of a great deal of paperwork. *Sooter* was very grateful to the Open Space Institute for their organizational support.

In terms of organizing, *Sooter* explained that they held small meetings in people's homes. At these meetings, activists would make presentations about the cement plant to small groups, which allowed Friends of Hudson to deliver their talking points in a setting that included their friends. *Sooter* told me that his group did several hundred of these meetings throughout the Hudson River Valley. He noted that these meetings forged social capital.

Additionally, *Sooter* explained that they also "did all the usual stuff: t-shirts and even 'swat the plant' fly swatters . . . To my everlasting regret, the one piece of paraphernalia that we didn't ever produce . . . a snow globe . . . all of the snow would be black. And we'd sell it for like $20 apiece as a fundraising device." He declared that even though this was very serious, activists still had fun. They also held other events to gather people.

Sooter recalled that the group had a picnic and dance every year it was active at the local Polish Sportsmen's Club. He stated, "Somebody said if you're going to have a revolution, you got to dance." He also told me of how their own research and a Rotary Club meeting where a cement plant representative spoke played to the Friends of Hudson's favor.

Sooter noted that his group discovered that cement plants burn hazardous waste to fuel operations. He explained that fuel to operate a plant is one-third of the production cost of cement. And he noted that corporations are able to acquire and burn hazardous waste for free, or even at a surplus. As such, it is often their goal to use this waste as fuel, which includes chemicals and old tires, among other things. *Sooter* argued that cement kilns are not an effective way to dispose of hazardous waste, and the by-product that is released from the smokestack will be spread over a two hundred–mile radius. After they discovered this information, they learned that the person in charge of leading the campaign to build the plant was going to be speaking at a local Rotary Club meeting.

Sooter recalled that his group attended the luncheon and, during the question period, inquired if the cement plant would burn hazardous waste. The representative said it would not. In response to the negative answer, *Sooter* asked if the cement plant representative would, through a legal mechanism, agree that the plant would never burn hazardous waste. *Sooter* recalled that the representative did not agree to that and the local business community did not take kindly to that answer. He noted that this was really the seminal moment in their efforts to defeat the plant. *Sooter* explained that as a result of this Rotary luncheon, and the response of the cement plant representative, a local businessperson who ran a factory that employed three hundred people wrote an editorial declaring his opposition to the plant. *Sooter* said that this was a key moment for the campaign.

Supervisor Linda Mussmann's words help explain why this moment had such impact. She recalled, "A lot of the people had ties to the cement plant of yesterday and it was a very emotional thing. And then it was an us versus them situation and people were deeply resentful of the antique dealers. They were resentful of the newcomers." Supervisor Mussmann recounted that residents whose family lived in Hudson for several generations saw the people trying to defeat the plant as different from themselves, whose forefathers worked in industry along the Hudson. She noted that the days of their grandparents were gone and the by-product being released from the smokestack was so small "it would embed itself in your lungs."

Supervisor Mussmann stated that her first electoral campaign came about as a result of this proposal. She remembered the challenge of that campaign. Supervisor Mussmann recalled, "First of all I was an outsider, secondly, a gay woman. Third, I'm against the plant. Chances of winning, it was an uphill battle." Mussmann also noted that the corporation pushing for the plan worked to divide residents and told local residents that the plant would be a way to drive the antique dealers out of Hudson. She noted that the corporation worked hard to make opposition to the plant look like elitism. But the efforts of *Sooter*, Mussmann, and a host of others paid off in the end.

The New York Department of State, through its jurisdiction over the State Coastal Management Program, made the final determination on the project (New York Department of State n.d.a). *Sooter* affirmed that New York's environmental review process was very helpful in defeating the plant. In particular, *Sooter* mentioned the State Environmental Quality Review Act, known as SEQRA (New York Department of State n.d.). SEQRA is an administrative review and approval process for projects that have an environmental impact. *Sooter* explained that SEQRA ensures a standardized process of reviewing these types of projects, overseen by an administrative law judge. *Sooter* praised the judge and also noted how appreciative he was that the residents of the state of New York have the ability to be a part of the review process.

Sooter explained that the cement company spent $59 million on the review. They then asked the Department of State for a determination on their project. The agency wrote a ruling that did not approve the plant for a number of reasons, including negative economic and visual effects, as well as blasting in a quarry. He noted that this occurred during the Pataki administration but credits the workers at the Coastal Management Program for defeating the plant.

Sooter took pride in this accomplishment because it empowered local residents. That said, he lamented, "And as good as we were, and as strong as we were as a citizen's group, you still have this concern that the powers that be are ultimately going to get their way. Because that's just what we're conditioned to be. That we're just peasants and the deal is going to happen in a dark hallway up in Albany somewhere or Jack's Supper Club near the capitol." Beyond the fact that these data illustrate that there is a robust progressive presence in the Hudson Valley and outside of major American cities, the stories also reveal that these activists played an important part in the policymaking process. But the narrative around the cement plant reveals other important information.

First, progressives know how to organize. That is not new. That is clear from other parts of this chapter. Second, progressives use a variety of means to achieve their policy goals. These include the ability to perform research, raise money, hire experts, educate the public, and run for public office. Many of these tools would be used in other successful environmental battles that Hudson Valley progressives fought.

And progressive activists in Hudson fought the status quo of corporate influence to work to achieve environmental equity and equal opportunity, by protecting the residents of Hudson from the negative impacts of this plant. Further, they formed a nonprofit and used it to convince government to prevent the cement plant from opening its doors.

Desalination Plant in Rockland County

A number of subjects from Rockland County spoke about their efforts to stop a water desalination plant. They used a variety of methods to organize around this issue.

Susanne and Dean Kernan explained the project in detail. Susanne reported that the desalination plant was proposed to be constructed three miles south of Indian Point, which is a maturing ground for Atlantic sturgeon. Susanne articulated that through her research, she found that desalination is an extremely expensive means of manufacturing drinking water since it requires a great deal of electricity and that New York has the highest electricity costs in the nation. Susanne revealed that wells located in Ramapo are the chief source of water for over three million Hudson Valley residents. She also divulged that drinking water became a concern in the early 2000s due to a few summers of drought. Government was also concerned about providing an adequate water supply.

Susanne informed me that the Department of Environmental Conservation required that the company guarantee there is enough water for residents in their plans. She made clear that a desalination plant would bring them more than double the return that they normally received back on an investment. The Kernans informed me that the desalination plant would impact sewer systems in the region, and Haverstraw would have been forced to upgrade its sewer system. Further, this would hurt the sturgeon who rely on the salinity level in the Hudson River.

Additionally, Dean Kernan explained, "Indian Point was given its license for operation with specific understanding that there would be no water pickups in the Hudson River below where Indian Point was. So, no drinking water was being taken out of the river." Susanne stated that the desalination process leaves tritium in the water. Further, the plan would have cost consumers far more money. She noted that costs to residential and commercial consumers would double if the plant was built. Progressives participated in a number of actions to defeat the desalination plant.

Alan Levin said that the effort to defeat the plant included large community meetings, signing petitions against the plant, and a great deal of contact with elected officials. Dolores Baldasare expressed that she distributed leaflets to defeat the plant. Jacquelyn Drechsler told me that she circulated brochures urging residents to attend a hearing on the issue. Drechsler also gave out literature at public places like ball fields. Jacquelyn also noted that small businesses were involved since this affected them; in particular, local restaurants helped fund experts to testify on behalf of those who wished to see the plant defeated. Drechsler also noted that she organized "Rockland's Got Talent" to defeat the plant. She also brought a ribbon campaign to Rockland on the issue. Drechsler proclaimed, "So, it's just coming up with unique ways of reaching people. But I do actually really just try to inform people."

Dean and Susanne Kernan explained that there was a coalition of interest groups involved in the battle. Dean told me that River Keeper, the Rockland Water Coalition, and the Sierra Club were part of this coalition. And these activists did research. Dean recalled that this coalition was able to bring together a broad group of volunteers, from the grassroots efforts to the professional scientists. Dean recalled that activists were heavily involved in monitoring legal agreements and scientific data, such as water flow rates. He recalled that these informed activists highlighted "that the regional drought, which sparked the whole thing for the new water supply . . . was manufactured by [the company], by them sending a lot of water down to New Jersey."

Susanne Kernan remembered that the Great Recession changed the demand for water and that the company used numbers based on consumption prior to the recession. Susanne recited a litany of commercial activities that have either left the area or substantially reduced their water usage. She noted that six of the top ten water consumers in the region before the recession were no longer in New York. Dean and Susanne both talked about town meetings, noting that in the middle of the week, both gatherings had over one thousand attendees each.

Jacquelyn Drechsler noted that 1,600 people came to the New York State Public Service Commission (PSC) hearing on the issue, which was noteworthy. Even so, Susanne remembered that opponents were not making the progress they hoped. She disclosed that another local activist became engaged in the campaign and directed what Dean called "the public advocacy part." Susanne noted that they used social media and collected twenty-five thousand petition signatures against the plant. This activist then organized a press conference, with boxes of petitions featured at the event in Albany. Susanne recalled, "The PSC was blown away. The DEC was blown away." Susanne remembered that the first thing stated by the officials was that the community engagement and activism against the plan was unprecedented, and that their activism stopped the plant. Susanne told me that this victory for progressives was featured prominently in *The New York Times*, primarily because it is a rarity for community coalitions to defeat corporations. She also thought that the company was stunned by the decision. There was also another element that illustrates, in Dean's words, "where the policy and politics joined."

The Kernans explained that a local town supervisor, who had the backing of his town Democratic committee, was supportive of the desalination plant. Their friend told the supervisor that she was going to run against the supervisor in a Democratic primary if he continued to support the plant. The Kernans recounted that the supervisor thought their friend was joking about the primary. Susanne recalled that this supervisor was a long-term incumbent.

Dean noted, "And that was a bare knuckles campaign. That was as ugly as it gets in local politics." Susanne recalled, "We got him to spend $100,000 against our $10,000 for an incumbent on a primary . . . But we got 39 percent of the vote. We scared him to death. And he backed off of the desal plant." Susanne stated that after a decade, the United States Geological Survey assessed the aquifers once more and determined that a drought was not looming.

It is clear that progressives employed a variety of tools to defeat the desalination plant. They raised funds, educated the public, held events, hired experts to testify against the plant, gathered petitions, held press conferences, and leveraged social media. And they even primaried an incumbent who supported the plant, causing him to spend $100,000 to defend his nomination. Further, the state recognized their unprecedented grassroots opposition to the plant. Clearly, progressives are visible in the Hudson Valley and are found in areas outside of America's largest cities. And they used government and nonprofits to fight the status quo of corporate dominance to provide environmental equity to the residents of the Hudson Valley and protect them from the negative impact of this plant.

GASIFICATION PLANT

Alan Levin and Gina I. each spoke about efforts among Rockland County progressives to prevent a gasification plant from being built in the town of Stony Point. They both noted the great deal of coalition building among different groups that occurred during this policy battle. Levin recalled that a number of environmental groups, including the Sierra Club, were involved. Gina I. noted that the Rockland Citizens Action Network was the platform activists used to organize and advocate against the plant. In addition to coalition building among various nonprofits, progressives conducted research while making their case to the public.

Dr. Gregory Julian, who lives in Stony Point, led the effort to stop the gasification plant. He reported that the plant would transport 4,500 tons of garbage from the five boroughs to Stony Point in Rockland County, where it would be manufactured into pellets through a gasification process. He continued, "But the pellets then were going to go into a refining process and chemically take the carbon and other chemicals . . . and create diesel fuel. And that diesel fuel would then have to be refined at another site. And the ash that it developed would be put into a fourth site." Dr. Julian insisted this process would take Stony Point backward and make it "a heavy industrialized town again." Thus, Dr. Julian began organizing the successful effort to stop the plant.

He recalled that they were able to prevent the gasification plant from being built. The site that the complex would have been constructed on had been used as an industrial site in the past, and activists interviewed retired employees of those industries. They discovered that the site was already a toxic waste site, and they learned not only that chemicals were buried there, but the exact locations of those chemicals. As such, the owner did not pursue the project. Dr. Julian explained, "We really researched the hell out of it." Dr. Julian revealed how they engaged the public to rally around defeating the plant.

Efforts included organizing large public meetings that had hundreds of attendees at each. Dr. Julian noted that roughly two weeks following the last meeting, the owner of the land decided not to pursue the plant. Julian noted that there were a number of narratives floating as to what was going through the minds of the corporate leaders.

Alan Levin believes that opposition from the community was the major factor that led to the owners dropping the project. Dr. Julian understands it might have to do with where chemicals were buried on the proposed site of the gasification plant. He recalled that after opponents learned where chemicals were buried on the site, they planned to contact the Department of Environmental Conservation and ask the agency to forcefully pursue the matter to remove those chemicals. Doing so would be an extremely costly affair.

Importantly, Dr. Julian expressed that the opponents of the plant formed a new grand coalition that included activists from a cross section of progressive groups such as the Sierra Club, MoveOn, environmental justice groups, voting rights groups, women groups, and elected officials. Julian proudly proclaimed, "Now this was really democracy at work. This is really what town halls could be if the citizens ran them . . . And based on research we got . . . there was so much information that it was so incriminating. The amount of carbon put into the air. The amount of methane put into the air. It was just astounding." Indeed, progressives were a prominent part of this policy battle.

While there is no evidence that explains exactly why the company that proposed the plant stopped the process, it is hard to imagine that the efforts by local progressives did not influence the corporation's decision. Progressives formed coalitions, conducted research, and mobilized. Indeed, they were not going to make the professional lives of those who wanted to build the plant enjoyable. It certainly illustrates that there is a robust progressive presence in the Hudson Valley and in areas beyond our biggest cities; and while linkages might be clearer, it suggests that they were prominent actors in the policy arena.

Further, the host of nonprofit coalition partners that the opposition to the plant included demonstrates that progressives use nonprofits to fight the status quo in support of environmental equity and equal opportunity. Progressives did not want both Stony Point and Haverstraw to bear the inequitable environmental burden associated with hosting this plant.

Ash Dump

Bart Sooter told me that a company was interested in establishing an ash dump in the town of Catskill, very close to the Hudson River. *Sooter* explained, "And of course one of the good things is that the experience built what is effectively a citizens coalition in this county and this region of the Hudson Valley; so now when an issue pops up, we can be in touch instantly with a large coalition of folks who might be interested and want to be engaged in it." *Sooter* continued, explaining the impressive resistance opponents of the plan were able to mount, which led the company to abandon their plans for the ash dump. Indeed, here is yet another example of progressives banding together to stop a project. In particular, this project required approval from the local town.

Ellen Schorsch of Greene County explained the plan more thoroughly. She told me that the company moves ashes that are produced from incinerators to an area that becomes a dump. The particular area that they wished to turn into an ash dump in Greene County was a quarry, and the stone is semiporous. This proposed dump is located roughly half a mile from the Hudson River. Ellen remembered that there was opposition not only in the county but also in many communities down river who rely on the Hudson as their main source of drinking water. Concerning this project, Roff wrote that the company would take ash and "dump it into a craggy, shifting quarry lined with a plastic sheet and pretend the liner sufficed to protect the Hudson River—just 2,500 feet away at the nearest point—and underground streams and groundwater" (2019). Roff revealed that over one hundred thousand individuals who use the Hudson as their drinking water supply would be affected by this plan. Clearly, this was a regional issue.

Efforts to stop the project started in April of 2018 (Roff 2019). Roff told readers that there were over fifty groups opposed to the plan, two hundred were signatures on a letter to the town supervisor opposing the dump, and almost three hundred attended the first community gathering about the proposal. In light of this resistance, by June 12, the company withdrew its request for a DEC permit.

Schorsch expressed that progressives were an important part of the opposition, but not the only opposition. She reflected, "And it's been real. Every day is a civics lesson for me. And I'm just so impressed with what can be done on a local level. Environmentally we can do a lot of things here . . . we need people who are willing to take a stand and work for the local communities." Progressives did not act alone.

The actions of progressives and their partners appeared to be disturbing to the company. And this story continues to show that progressives build coalitions to stop policy proposals that they find troubling. Further, this narrative continues to illustrate that there is a robust progressive presence in the Hudson Valley and its policy arena, and that progressives are not simply found in America's largest cities. Further, progressives used government and nonprofit groups to fight the status quo of corporate power to provide environmental equity and equal opportunity. Indeed, they worked to protect residents of the Hudson Valley, particularly those who receive their drinking water from the river, from being disproportionately affected by this project.

ASSESSMENT OF PROGRESSIVES STOPPING POLICY

It should come as no surprise that each of the policy proposals that progressives successfully stopped all had severe environmental impacts. First, the cement plant, the desalination plant, the gasification plant, and the ash dump would impact people in the surrounding area and the Hudson River itself. Second, in each of these instances, progressives were a part of a coalition that included nonprofit entities. They brought people together to stop policy. Beyond this, progressives were actively engaged in educating the public and bringing awareness to the consequences of each proposal. They often performed research and raised funds for experts to help them in their quests. In one instance, they even challenged a pro-project incumbent in a primary election.

Generally, it was clear how progressives directly stopped a policy from being adopted. In some instances, the cause and effect were murkier. That said, the data suggest that progressives were a factor in each of these policy decisions. And, just as importantly, these stories show us that there is a robust progressive presence in the Hudson Valley and in areas outside of America's most densely populated urban areas. Finally, progressives used government and nonprofits to fight for environmental equity and equal opportunity by not allowing these projects to disproportionately impact communities in the region.

Failing to Realize the Adoption of Desired Policy Solutions

Progressive activists in the Hudson Valley have a good record of seeing their desired policy solutions adopted and unwanted policy proposals defeated.

But they are not always successful in their policy quests. They often run into strong headwinds from those who wish to maintain the status quo. Campaign finance reform in Dutchess County and a living wage bill in Rockland County are two examples of this reality. Importantly, these exemplars clearly illustrate that progressives use government and nonprofit entities to fight the status quo in their desire to bring about equity and equal opportunity. And the narratives continue to reveal a robust progressive presence in the region.

CAMPAIGN FINANCE REFORM

Activists affiliated with the Dutchess County Progressive Action Alliance were involved in a number of reform efforts. One of the most prominent was their quest to reform campaign finance rules for candidates seeking county office in Dutchess County.

Caroline Fenner of Dutchess County recalled that she wanted to start working on a local issue after Donald Trump was elected, and, after some thought, found that campaign finance reform meant the most to her. Fenner drafted ideas and presented them at a meeting of the Dutchess County Legislature.

Caroline explained that she had never been to a meeting of the county legislature and, despite feeling nervous, stood up and spoke about the need for campaign finance reform. Fenner recounted, "After I spoke, about three Republicans and maybe four Democrats came up and congratulated me . . . saying they agreed with me, that we need campaign finance reform in Dutchess County. So that felt good, and it did feel to me like okay, this could happen. This is going to be easy. No, not at all." Fenner described the beginning of her work on this issue. She emailed legislators every day to remind them about the issue and performed a great deal of research in order to build momentum. And a bill was introduced. Caroline told me that a Democratic legislator and a Republican legislator each cosponsored a campaign finance reform bill. That said, a county attorney believed it was illegal for a municipality to make campaign finance laws.

Caroline recalled that she pushed back on this assertion, pointing out that, beside New York City, local campaign finance laws were passed and not challenged by the state in Rockland, Orange, and Suffolk Counties. Caroline noted that the GOP majority refused to allow the bill to go to committee to be discussed. Fenner explained, "And that was a big red signal to me that there are many people benefiting directly from the way it is right now. And they are lining their pockets with money from corporations inside Dutchess County and outside Dutchess County, who are basically setting up a pay-to-play situation." Caroline told me about her next steps. A petition drive was launched—where over one thousand signatures were gathered in support of campaign finance reform that came from across the county. Caroline told me that she delivered the petitions and then the issue seemed to be dead. There was no movement from the legislature.

But Caroline and her fellow progressives did not stop the fight. They honed their message and called for public financing of campaigns for county positions. Fenner explained that they sought input from an expert on the issue from Democracy Matters to launch another petition drive. They then circulated that petition. Caroline explained that she also worked with a county legislator on drafting another resolution. Maria Quackenbush explained more about their newer campaign finance petition.

Maria reported that the wording of this second petition is important because they had the county executive at the time explaining that public financing of elections is the major route to realizing political change in county government. Maria asserted, "So, we're calling him on it." Maria continued, noting that the petition mirrors his words. Maria also explained her engagement with the public on the issue.

She recalled some of her petition-gathering efforts. She noted that everyone she asked to sign the petition did so, particularly those from lower socioeconomic backgrounds. Maria recounted that these residents even brought their friends to sign the petition. "So, don't tell me they wouldn't be on board if they thought it was going to make a difference," Maria asserted. As of this writing, the proposal has not become law.

Progressives employed the nonprofit Dutchess County Progressive Action Alliance as a hub to attempt to bring about reform. Despite an organized, well-researched attempt with support from sitting legislators, the majority party in the county legislature prevented any action on campaign finance reform. That said, two important points should be noted. First, there is clearly a robust progressive presence in the region and in areas beyond America's largest urban municipalities. Second, progressives used nonprofits and government to attempt to bring about equity and equal opportunity. Indeed, changing the way campaigns are financed would break down many barriers and would allow individuals with fewer resources to launch viable campaigns for public office. Further, it is feasible that public financing of campaigns would change the dynamics of the legislative process, potentially opening a path for ordinances to be adopted that may bring about equity and equal opportunity that previously had no feasible path forward.

It should be no surprise, given the writing in this chapter, that progressives were involved in other attempts to raise the minimum wage or establish a living wage.

Steven White explained his efforts to realize a living wage ordinance in Rockland County, working with a member of the Rockland County Legislature at the time. This effort was part of the work of the Rockland Coalition for Peace and Justice. White continued, telling me that the county legislature passed the resolution, but the Republican county executive vetoed the bill. In order to override the veto, a supermajority would be required, and White noted that they fell one vote short of achieving this threshold on two occasions. White thought, but could not prove, that something underhanded was happening to prevent the passage of the bill. Thus, White believed one of the legislators prevented the ordinance from passing.

Jen Fuentes gave a similar story about her time on the Kingston Common Council. She explained that one of her first actions on the council was to write to Governor Andrew Cuomo, along with other elected officials spread throughout New York, urging him to raise the minimum wage through administrative mechanisms. Other legislators, she recalled, criticized her for doing that because they said it placed them "in a vulnerable spot." Sometimes, political headwinds are just too much to overcome for progressive activists.

That said, these stories clearly illustrate that there is a robust progressive presence in the Hudson Valley and throughout regions beyond America's biggest urban areas. And they attempted to leverage nonprofits, such as the Rockland Coalition for Peace and Justice, and government to fight the status quo and bring about policies that could usher in equity and equal opportunity.

Assessment of Failing to Realize the Adoption of Desired Policy Solutions

The progressive activists in this study are true believers. They also know the manner of how public policy is manufactured in New York. They knew exactly which officials could adopt their desired policy solutions. And, yet, they too ran into the cold, hard reality of power dynamics in each of these instances. Nevertheless, these activists engaged with policymakers.

Caroline Fenner had legislation introduced in the Dutchess County Legislature. Steven White recounted that legislation passed, but that there was not enough support to override the county executive's veto. Nevertheless, the fact that legislation was considered illustrates that, first, there is a robust progressive presence in the Hudson Valley and in regions beyond our largest urban cities. And, second, progressives are prominent members of the policymaking arena in the region.

Further, nonprofits, including the Dutchess County Progressive Action Alliance and the Rockland Coalition for Peace and Justice, were conduits through which progressive activists worked to persuade government officials to adopt policies that would advance a march toward equity and equal opportunity.

The last part of this chapter will explore several policy proposals that progressives unsuccessfully worked to defeat.

Failing to Stop Undesired Policy Proposals

As this chapter already noted, progressive political activists spend a great deal of time working to defeat policy proposals that they find to be problematic. And they were successful in many of their quests. That said, they were not always effective at preventing the adoption of policies and projects they find troubling. This section will highlight some of those efforts.

Environmental

It should be no surprise, given what we learned about progressive political activists thus far, that progressives work to protect the environment from policies and projects that they deem problematic. And it should further come as no surprise that much of their time is found working to defeat proposals that they find to be environmentally detrimental. But, unlike previous efforts outlined in this chapter, they were not always successful.

Pramilla Malick told me about a proposed hazardous project in her town. She noted, "It was a private project to benefit a private corporation but completely dependent on public resources and encroached upon the rights of the public." Malick argued that global corporate entities are essentially "colonizing" pockets of the United States, which she noted is nothing new, and destroying local communities in the process by draining both liberties and assets from these areas. Further, these actions also damage municipal power. Pramilla Malick explained that while they were not successful in stopping an environmentally damaging project from taking place, residents of other areas were successful at stopping corporations based on the tactics Malick employed. Pramilla Malick explained that her community engaged with the Federal Energy Regulatory Commission. Malick and her community's efforts included protesting, attending agency hearings, and lobbying the commission. Malick told me this was the first time community members who were dealing with an unwanted project in their neighborhoods engaged with this body. But they were unsuccessful at stopping this project. This was not the only project Hudson Valley progressives were unsuccessful at curtailing.

Dr. Barbara Kidney lamented about pipelines and power plants coming through the region. Regarding a plant that is already operating, Dr. Kidney reported that residents have been complaining about noxious fumes permeating throughout their homes and many experienced headaches as a result. Further, she noted that birds, including bald eagles, have been negatively affected.

Regarding another project, Dr. Kidney informed me that a proposed power plant is "supposed to add 25 percent more greenhouse gas emissions." Caroline Fenner explained more about the proposed power plant.

Caroline made known that the environment team of Dutchess County Progressive Action Alliance opposed the project. She asserted that gas produced from fracking is used in the plant, noting that the gas originated in Pennsylvania. Fenner explained that DCPAA's environment action team has been highly engaged with educating the public about the plant, "and the incredible amounts of known and unknown contaminants that will spew from the plant and . . . affect the local environment and the people, especially the schoolchildren."

Fenner described the actions that local activists took to stop the plant. She stated that an action team that started with Dutchess County Progressive Action Alliance that solely focused on the proposed plant left the organization and became an independent entity since the group is so focused on one issue. Fenner reported that this group also pickets and attends community meetings. As of this writing, the plant that these activists opposed is operating.

These narratives tell us that despite not being able to stop several environmental projects, progressives are still actively engaged in the Hudson Valley and found outside of America's largest cities. Their presence is certainly clear. Further, Pramilla Malick's story explaining that other communities around the country used her efforts with the Federal Energy Regulatory Commission as a model to successfully stop other projects illustrates that progressives can make a policy impact. And, importantly, progressives used nonprofits like the Dutchess County Progressive Action Alliance and government entities like the Federal Energy Regulatory Commission to attempt to stop policy paths that lead to inequity and curtail equal opportunity. In fact, in 2021, the Federal Energy Regulatory Commission announced the establishment of an Office of Public Participation, which Senator Jeanne Shaheen asserts, "is a victory for the public and will help ensure they play a strong role in shaping our nation's energy future" (Shaheen 2021). Certainly, individuals who were experiencing negative impacts from these plants must feel that they have been treated inequitably and have had their equal opportunity to live peaceful lives curtailed. Progressives were engaged in attempts to stop other projects that fall outside of the environmental realm.

GREENE COUNTY JAIL

All four subjects from Greene County lamented that they could not stop their county legislature from authorizing the construction of a new jail. Carolyn M. Riggs reported that the cost of the project was over $47 million. She stated that she does not believe the county can afford this expenditure. Riggs noted that when the project was first introduced, Republicans held a six-seat majority on the fourteen-member county legislature; and now, they hold a ten-seat majority. Dr. Ron Lipton indicated that the state told Greene County that the jail was "uninhabitable, and they had to do something about it."

Dustin Reidy from Albany explained that a number of Greene County residents wanted to merge the Columbia and Greene County jails, but he highlighted the pride many residents had in keeping the county jail local. Dr. Lipton told me that the county is receiving a loan from the United States Department of Agriculture for the jail, and "under the guise of helping rural communities, they have funded many jails." Greene County was awarded a $39 million loan from the Department of Agriculture for the project; they then issued bonds in that amount to cover the cost of the loan (Greene County, New York 2019). Dr. Lipton noted that former US representative John Faso helped to secure the loan.

Reidy and Dr. Lipton both explained that Mountain Top Progressives was heavily involved in opposition to the jail. Dr. Lipton noted that group members were leaders in the unsuccessful effort to stop the jail. Ellen Schorsch and Jonathan Gross, leaders of Mountain Top Progressives, recounted their organization's efforts.

Jonathan reported that his group, Mountain Top Progressives, organized a committee to stop the jail, which he asserted helped launch an organized movement against the jail that included others beyond members of Mountain Top Progressives. Jonathan recalled that the movement gained traction because residents did not understand how pursuing the project at the cost projection was commonsensical. Jonathan observed, "We started that committee and it blossomed into Greene County good government and stop the jail, and it became a huge movement. It started because we started it, and it grew."

Ellen Schorsch told me that members of her group attended meetings of the Greene County Legislature to advocate on behalf of not spending money to construct a new jail. She recounted that they had no qualms about speaking up against the proposal. Jonathan asserted, "It was American grassroots politics at its most beautiful and also its ugliest, both combined. It really was. There's something going on that we can't figure out. There was so much obstruction." Gross argued that building a new jail is perplexing since it currently has twenty-eight inmates and that number keeps falling.

Ellen Schorsch observed that contracts for the project originated outside of Greene County and that no one in Greene County gained employment from these contracts. Schorsch also recalled that while the land for the site was given by the state, it will cost the county $8.5 million to connect utilities to the site. Jonathan asserted that this money could be spent on other pressing social service needs in the county that would attract businesses and people to buy property in the county. Mountain Top Progressives also tried to change the law in Albany, allowing for Greene County and neighboring Columbia County, who already share some core services, to build a shared jail together.

Ellen told me that they advocated for a law in Albany that permitted Greene County to provide for jail services in conjunction with surrounding counties. The bills were introduced in the state assembly (New York State Assembly 2019) and the state senate (New York State Assembly 2019a). The bill in the assembly passed through the correction committee but did not go further (New York State Assembly 2019). The bill in the senate was referred to the local government committee, where it was not considered at all (New York State Assembly 2019a). Thus, activists ran into political reality at the Greene County legislative chamber and in the New York State Capitol. Ultimately, they were not able to stop the jail.

Nevertheless, it is clear that there was a robust progressive presence in the Hudson Valley, focused by Mountain Top Progressives, on this issue. It should be clearly stated that Greene County is an extremely rural county, pointing once again to the fact that progressives are found in areas outside of America's largest cities. They were actively engaged in the county policy arena and also saw bills to support their efforts appear in both chambers of the New York State Legislature. Thus, despite not realizing what they would consider to be a success, progressives in Greene County still put up a prominent and valiant effort.

Further, it was clearly noted that they thought the money could be far better used on "recovery services, mental health services, more family court," per Gross. These are policies that could be used to bring about greater equity and equal opportunity. And they used Mountain Top Progressives, a nonprofit group, to press government to fight the status quo.

Assessment of Failing to Stop Undesired Policy Proposals

Progressives work to defeat policy proposals that they find problematic. And, to do so, they usually work with other progressives. Indeed, groups like Dutchess County Progressive Action Alliance, Mountain Top Progressives, and Rockland Citizens Action Network serve as organizing hubs for progressive activists throughout the Hudson Valley. Progressives know how to organize.

These efforts also illustrate one other important point: progressive activists have a command of the roles and powers of government agencies that few possess. Pramilla Malick knew to approach the Federal Energy Regulatory Commission, which until then had operated entirely in the shadows, accessible only to industry insiders. Ellen Schorsch and Jonathan Gross understood that this policy could be curtailed either through local ordinance or by state legislation. And, in each of these instances, local progressives advocated their position.

Even if they were unsuccessful in each of these battles from a policy standpoint, they were considered. They were a noticeable part of the policy arena. Indeed, there is a robust progressive presence in the Hudson Valley and outside of America's largest cities. And these progressives are a visible and important part of the policymaking arena.

Conclusion

These exemplars show five policy areas, all involving reserved and concurrent powers, where progressives helped to manufacture policy and stop undesired policy solutions. And it is also important to illustrate that progressives are not always successful. They do not always see their desired policy proposals come to fruition. And they did not constantly possess the tools and muscle to stop the adoption of proposals that they found damaging. This is simply the way policymaking works.

That said, progressives use a variety of tools in their policy efforts. They know which policymakers to approach about a particular issue. Whether they need to work with a city council or town board, county legislature, state legislature, or an obscure public authority—progressives understand the details of government policymaking. This point should not be overlooked. They are a civically educated group.

And progressives know how to talk to individual policymakers. Jason Angell clearly had the attention of municipal policymakers in his quest to adopt Community Choice Aggregation. Caroline Fenner worked with two members of the Dutchess County Legislature on a campaign finance bill. Ellen Schorsch and Jonathan Gross saw their effort taken up by state legislators. Even if these bills did not pass, they were still introduced. This should not go unnoticed. *Bart Sooter* and his group were certainly considered by the New York Department of State. The extensive effort to pass resolutions against the Pilgrim Pipeline were on the minds of municipal officials. And the manner of how Tasha Young approached a local school district to change the school-to-prison pipeline is novel and inspiring.

In other instances, progressives made policy themselves. The efforts of Dr. Gregory Julian to integrate schools during his tenure as a school board president are remarkable and heartening. The work of Jen Fuentes as an appointed official in Kingston and Ginny O'Brien as an elected official in East Greenbush on parks is notable.

The use of the party structure and the system of fusion voting is striking. Working Families Party state committeeman David Schwartz leveraged his influence to help raise the minimum wage statewide. His story is remarkable. It shows the confluence of politics and policy in an extremely realistic manner that is familiar to New York voters whose electoral system allows fusion voting.

Progressives know how to assemble a critical mass of voters, generally large enough for policymakers to consider their demands. And a key part of this is civic education. Progressives are civic educators. They teach the mass public about policy issues and are able to assemble citizens that they teach about issues to either support or oppose proposed policies. They are able to marshal large numbers of voters to attend hearings and testify before their own legislators.

And when they are bothered by the position of an elected official, they run for office. Linda Mussmann first sought office because of her opposition to the proposed cement plant. A town supervisor in Rockland spent $100,000 defeating his anti-desalination plant opponent in a primary contest.

Progressives raise money, like Jacquelyn Drechsler with Rockland's Got Talent, or, *Sooter's* group raising $2.5 million in their effort to stop the cement plant. And they used this cash to hire experts. Progressives bring people together, whether in action teams like on the mountaintop of Greene County, or sitting with coffee and donuts listening to a presentation on a cement plant.

Indeed, in line with the overarching thesis of this project, progressives are robustly involved in the policy process and have a strong presence throughout the Hudson Valley. And their activism shows that progressives are found outside of America's largest cities, including in rural Greene County. They engage policymakers, activists, and the community at large. Further, they use government and nonprofit entities to fight the status quo in support of policies that they believe will usher in equity and equal opportunity—whether these policies are environmental, economic, electoral, or otherwise.

The next chapter will look at other civic activities of progressives that do not necessarily fall into electoral activities or policymaking activities. Nevertheless, they engage the community. As such, their robust presence continues to be evident from their activities.

Chapter 5

Progressives and Other Civic Activities

There is a robust and diverse progressive presence in the Hudson Valley. The evidence put forward in the preceding two chapters highlights their important roles in the political party structure, in campaigns and elections, and in the policymaking arena. This chapter will provide readers with two things.

First, it will illustrate some very important efforts of progressives that do not fall neatly into either electoral activities or policymaking. Second, it will highlight their efforts to engage and inform the public. While these latter exertions may orbit the realms of policymaking and elections, their activities around these areas are so robust that they deserve exploration and explanation in their own right in this constitutive analysis. Importantly, this will continue to illustrate that there is a diverse and robust progressive presence in New York's Hudson Valley. It follows then that progressives are not simply found in America's largest cities. Finally, progressives use governments and nonprofits to fight the status quo in the hope of bringing about equity and equal opportunity. This chapter largely focuses on progressive use of nonprofit entities.

Progressive Civic Endeavors

Progressives are active in a number of nonprofit civic organizations. These organizations are public-serving entities that engage residents of an area in a particular manner. Through these entities, progressives work to bring people into the civic process, or provide a service that government does not provide.

One of the most heartening activities that I learned about during my interviews is the Hudson Valley Community Congress. In a previous chapter, Jason Angell of Putnam County told me about his commitment to "radical localism." His efforts to engage citizens through the Hudson Valley Community Congress are indicative of a commitment to what political scientists refer to as "small d" democracy. Further, Angell's work also illustrates a devotion to sparking civic engagement.

Jason Angell explained that he and his wife were "just very disturbed" by the 2016 General Election. He recounted that following President Trump's victory, they opened their farm as a community meeting place for people to air their concerns, where around 180 individuals attended. Jason explained, "Part of our sadness was the feeling that we're in deep shit if that many Americans are so disgusted with the status quo that they are going to elect someone like Donald." He continued, asserting that so many Americans are just disgusted with politics as usual, partisanship, and the influence of corporations that they voted for Trump for drastic change.

Angell reported that the initial meetings became partisan and that he did not want to simply focus efforts on the next midterm election. In an effort to keep partisan politics outside of this endeavor, the nonprofit Hudson Valley Community Congress was formed to have local residents determine the policy areas where communities should focus their energies. He told me that in order to determine these areas, community members are given three minutes at a community meeting to promote their desired policy areas. After everyone spoke, community members ranked their top priorities and then these priorities were presented to their US representative. Angell declared, "And so it was very participatory democracy . . . it was about finding a way to create an agenda within the community." The Hudson Valley Community Congress created a space for people to express their views and an outlet to determine what they believe are the most important issues.

Beside the 2016 General Election, Angell lamented about what he believes are the systemic problems that are endemic in the American political system, most prominently, campaign donations and political parties. He also questioned if it is possible to reform the current system in a meaningful way. Angell insisted that electing a junior legislator who is simply one voice among many, and not in charge of any important committees, is simply not going to produce reform.

With this in mind, Angell reported that he organized a community congress in Philipstown in Putnam County and Peekskill in Westchester County. He also noted that it is completely nonpartisan and not connected to electoral politics. Angell expressed, "It's very much like *American Idol* meets democracy." They held three community meetings for people to identify a policy solution to strengthen their community. He clearly asserted that it is not simply a griping session, but there must be some action that can be taken to fix a problem. Angell told me that he finds the discussions entertaining. After the three-minute speeches, attendees socialize.

He stated that they work to bring various constituencies in a given community together and have them socialize. Angell expressed that the first two programs produced forty proposals. From there, Angell recounted that each and every proposal went on a ballot. Then, these ballots were mailed to each household in each given community, where people were instructed to rank their top three proposals. Angell explained that they worked hard to ensure people returned those ballots. From there, they count votes to determine the top three priorities. These priorities are then used to spark civic engagement, making sure elected officials know the opinions of community members. Per the group's website, a total of seventy-five local residents suggested a priority. In total, 2,284 ballots were cast to determine the top three priorities (Ecological Citizens n.d.).

Jason Angell articulated, "Divorce an idea from a political party; you just put it on a ballot without any political context. I think you can get surprising results." Jason recalled speaking to a group of men from a local shooting and hunting club. After receiving a great deal of pushback from its members, one of the men from the group expressed that he thought his town needed more biking infrastructure. Angell asserted that he firmly disagreed with this group's national policy positions, but taking an issue out of a partisan political context can produce shared policy goals, like a shared position on biking infrastructure. Per Angell, the Philipstown Community Congress then brought these issues to candidates running for county office.

Angell noted about 30 percent of residents who voted in the last municipal election in Philipstown cast ballots in the community congress. Angell also explained that the Republican county executive was not going to participate in any candidate forums in Philipstown since it is the county's Democratic stronghold. But the incumbent and her Democratic challenger, as well as county legislative candidates, participated in their community forum where they were asked how they will help find solutions to the policy problems that community congress members supported. Angell continued, explaining that this forum was different than a candidate giving their usual stump speech. Candidates needed to be more focused, identifying how they would use their power to address the issues identified by the community. "And so that was, to me, a victory because it was showing how different things could be in terms of getting elected officials to respond to their constituents," Angell declared. Indeed, even though this is not a partisan affair, the community congress had the attention of elected officials and candidates for public office.

Jason Angell is clearly an active voice in his community who works diligently to foster civic engagement. His actions and the labors of the organizers and volunteers of the Hudson Valley Community Congress illustrate a commitment to local democracy. Also, importantly, these efforts illustrate attention to the opinions and wishes of citizens.

A given area does not require progressive activists to launch and operate a community congress. That said, this organization was established and spearheaded by a prominent local progressive, Jason Angell. This is clearly a noteworthy exemplar illustrating a robust and important progressive presence in the Hudson Valley and outside of America's largest cities. Indeed, Angell is a farmer. Further, it demonstrates that progressives use nonprofits and government to attempt to bring about equity and equal opportunity. In particular, this effort shows representational equity and equal opportunity. Any local resident can speak for three minutes and have their project considered by fellow citizens.

The Hudson Valley Community Congress is not the only nonprofit that endeavors to hear directly from citizens about their policy needs and policy wants.

COMMUNITY VOICES HEARD

Terence Miller of Westchester County told me about his work with Community Voices Heard. Miller explained that the mission of the organization is to advocate for residents from low-income areas. Miller noted that in his role as a "member leader," he connects with community members to ask what issues and problems are important to them and determines how Community Voices Heard can help resolve these concerns. Further, he works to recruit people into the organization. In order to do this, Miller and other member leaders go door to door and engage residents to explore their problems. Miller observed, "Government constantly tells people what they're going to do for them but rarely does the government say what do you want from us; and I think that's where the contention is between people and the government." Miller is very clear in his belief that government should listen to the people it represents.

Miller also explained that the issues that are of concern to residents are not simply limited to common concerns that people living in low-income areas face, but the issues are linked to what residents want to address. Miller noted that it is an organization that is led by its membership. At the time of our meeting, housing was the biggest issue under consideration, per Miller. Terence was not the only subject who worked with Community Voices Heard. David Schwartz was extremely fond of the organization.

David Schwartz asserted, "I think the group I work most happily with and respect is Community Voices Heard." Schwartz noted, "They were founded to give voice to poor people of color. And Michael, they really give voice . . . it isn't a bunch of educated, white people telling . . . black people what they need." David recalled that just after the American Recovery and Reinvestment Act became law he went on a public housing bus tour in Yonkers that highlighted how stimulus money was used. He told me that he continuously told himself to stay quiet and listen. He said the money was used to plant flowers outside of a building. David explained that he initially thought the money could have been put to other uses, but then he came to the conclusion that it should not be up to him to decide. He recalled that he scolded himself and kept reminding himself to stay quiet and hear the local residents. Schwartz said again that this is his favorite organization. Community Voices Heard is another organization that works to engage people in the Hudson Valley.

Similar to the Hudson Valley Community Congress, Community Voices Heard's dedication to "small d" democracy is heartening. Further, and just as importantly, its activities continue to demonstrate that there is a robust progressive presence in the Hudson Valley and outside of America's largest cities, though clearly, Yonkers is an urban area. Also, Community Voices Heard illustrates that progressives are a robust part of the civic community at large. They use nonprofits and government to fight the status quo to advance representational equity and equal opportunity.

COLUMBIA COUNTY BAIL FUND

Prior to bail reform in New York, bail funds existed to help individuals who could not afford to post bail for committing misdemeanors. Supervisor Linda

Mussmann told me about the efforts of local progressives to establish a bail fund in Columbia County, noting that it was the only fund that existed upstate. This bail fund was a nonprofit entity that Mussmann revealed started in either 2017 or 2018.

Supervisor Mussmann reported that the fund was allowed to post bail—as long as the bail was not over $2,000—per state law. Mussmann observed that once these individuals were out of jail, they went back to their jobs, or were able to continue providing stability to their families. Mussmann addressed the notion that people who posted bail left the area. She was quick to point out that it is hard for a person to leave town if they do not have money to travel.

She stated, "So, it was a very progressive statement about how we felt about the criminal system, and on a local level, how we felt it could change. And doing that was a big deal. We bailed out about thirty people in the last two years." Mussmann, who works in nonprofits beyond her duties as an elected official, noted that donors were extremely willing to give to the bail fund, more so than any other organizations for which she raised money. Supervisor Mussmann recalled that they were able to raise funds fast and continuously have the cash needed to maintain the organization. Mussmann also noted that they would help people when they were in court.

Per the group's Facebook page, with bail reform in the works at the time of this interview, the group was likely to close the fund (Columbia County Bail Fund 2020). They stopped accepting donations in 2019 (Columbia County Bail Fund 2019). That said, meeting bail for thirty individuals in a relatively small county and establishing a nonprofit shows that there is a robust and diverse progressive presence in the Hudson Valley. Further, this organization clearly shows that progressives are active outside of America's largest urban areas.

This is indicative of progressives using nonprofit means to fight the status quo in order to provide economic equity and equal opportunity for those that committed misdemeanors. There are other nonprofit entities employed by progressives that also strive toward economic equity and equal opportunity.

Save Them Now and Business Alliance of Kingston

Pat Strong of Ulster County told me of her work with Save Them Now, a nonprofit organization that helped individuals who were recently released from incarceration. The organization offered, "transitional housing to Ulster

County men who have recently returned from prison or long-term treatment programs" (UlsterCorps 2009).

Strong observed that this was a novel program in Ulster County. She also noted that locals like to think that this population does not live in their communities, "but they're there and so we shined a light on that, and we brought a lot of public attention to it in the years that we ran that program." Pat Strong recounted her pride when Pete Seeger gave his support to the program and performed at a benefit for the organization. While this program is no longer active, Strong told me of other efforts to help those who recently left incarceration.

Strong explained her time working with the Business Alliance of Kingston, which she clearly notes does not sound like a progressive organization. Strong told me that this is a group of business owners in the city of Kingston who are involved in a number of local causes, from the arts, to environmental concerns, to small business advocacy. At the time of the interview, this group worked to help small businesses operate but also engage in important issues. Strong recounted that they were involved with a program sponsored by Ulster County Sheriff Juan Figueroa to provide job opportunities for people who were released from the Ulster County Jail. Strong continued, "He wants to help them find, as he calls it, a first chance in life. Not so much a second chance. He argues many of them haven't had first chances. So, we're developing a program where we would interview these young people coming out of incarceration and help them find employment." This is another example of progressives in the region using their influence to help meet a need, and to do so, by engaging small business owners in the community.

Indeed, the efforts of local progressives to help those who need help is further indicative of a robust progressive presence in the Hudson Valley's civic arena. Further, this is another exemplar that indicates the ability of progressives to engage citizens in the community outside of America's largest urban areas. These efforts continue to illustrate that progressives fight the status quo in the hope of advancing economic equity and equal opportunity. And they use nonprofits such as Save Them Now and the Business Alliance of Kingston in their attempts to provide equity and equal opportunity.

ASSET-BASED COMMUNITY DEVELOPMENT

Rev. Jordan Scruggs told me about her work with low-income communities in the city of Kingston. In our conversation, she lamented about the difficulties that gentrification is creating for low-income communities, including communities of color, in Kingston. Reverend Scruggs, whose job portfolio included poverty relief, noted that her job is to forge relationships between her church and the local community, particularly around mitigating poverty. As such, she believes it is vital to live in the community where she works. Part of her efforts include asset-based community development.

Reverend Scruggs observed, "Most of the time, capital flow in low-income communities is organized around deficits . . . you qualify for a program as a student if your parent has a drug addiction, or is a certain level below the median income." She explained that there are a number of families who barely do not qualify for these programs, but, if they experience one unexpected issue, like an illness, they fall below meeting their own needs. She noted that children in this group are largely ignored. Reverend Scruggs explained that asset-based community development invests in places that are maintaining themselves, in order to help the people in these communities become more prosperous and stable. She stated that this does not mean cutting government services but creating opportunity. This is organized through a nonprofit, Kingston Midtown Rising.

Reverend Scruggs offered some examples of this approach. She told me about a church in Midtown Kingston that is close to closing its doors. She is working with a local nonprofit to transform that building into a center of community that is planned by residents in the church's neighborhood "to create a space of opportunity."

Reverend Scruggs told me that this included afterschool programs that are not driven by income levels, but by leadership. This entails leadership by students who have the skills to make a difference in their classrooms in some way. She observed that if a student has enough influence in their schools to either derail a classroom, or transform it into something delightful, then they have leadership abilities and skills. Further, Reverend Scruggs asked how the community invests in students of color in the city of Kingston, who leave the area upon graduation because of a lack of opportunities. Thus, asset-based community development is an endeavor to "cultivate and create an environment where children build value as though they have something to contribute to their community, and it makes them want to stay here. And the same is true for adults," per Reverend Scruggs.

RUCPO, a local housing organization in Kingston, writes that asset-based community development seeks to "empower communities to guide their own decision making" and "improve development decision making in local communities" (RUPCO 2019). This strategy is another exemplar of a robust progressive presence in the Hudson Valley. Reverend Scruggs and those who are engaged in this effort bring about more "small d" democracy that we saw in other parts of this chapter by engaging the community. Indeed, progressives are a visible part of the civic community in the Hudson Valley and outside of America's largest cities. Further, progressives often are lambasted by conservatives for being secular. This is a clear example illustrating that progressives may even be ordained ministers. It also highlights the diversity of the progressive community. And it shows progressives leveraging nonprofit organizations to fight the status quo in the hope of moving toward equity and equal opportunity.

Islamic Community Center for Mid-Westchester

Dr. Charles Chesnavage, the president of the Westchester Coalition Against Islamophobia, told me about his coalition's effort to help the Islamic Community Center of Mid-Westchester (ICCMW). He explained that the ICCMW purchased a house in the Colonial Heights neighborhood of the city of Yonkers to employ as a mosque under the assumption that using the building as a house of worship would not conflict with zoning laws. Chesnavage recalled that a local neighborhood group worked to landmark the building following its acquisition by ICCMW. Chesnavage articulated that landmark status places administrative hurdles on the owners of a property. It prevents them from altering the outside of the structure once it is landmarked. Chesnavage reported that the landmark was approved unanimously by the landmark committee of the city of Yonkers, even over objections that the landmark was intolerant. He also found the unanimity of the declaration to be peculiar.

Chesnavage recounted that after the determination by the landmark committee, his group continued advocating against the landmark, even meeting with the mayor of Yonkers. Chesnavage explained that at the time of the decision, Republicans had a majority on the Yonkers City Council, who, on a party line vote, upheld the landmark determination. Chesnavage expressed appreciation for the support of the council Democrats in his effort. From there, the issue went to court, where the ICCMW has been unsuccessful.

Chesnavage reported that the courts did not find enough evidence that the landmark determination was based on discrimination. He also recalled that the lead attorney for the ICCMW believed the landmark determination violated the First Amendment. Chesnavage asserted, "And he was really basing it on that and in some precedent in previous cases. There was no need to present any further evidence, but the mere fact that group was creating an obstacle or making it difficult for them to proceed for religious reasons, that was enough." Jurists in the case, per Chesnavage, acknowledged that there were anti-Muslim sentiments expressed at some local meetings, but he did not believe there was enough concrete evidence to illustrate what the landmark status of the house denied the ICCMW.

Chesnavage reported, "These kinds of cases have been taking place again, locally, in Jersey, Connecticut, and around the country. There are strategies used by individuals that are anti-Muslim, more fearful of Muslims, which would constitute examples of Islamophobia. We feel that that was the case here." Chesnavage noted that there was turnover on the Yonkers City Council.

But, he explained, since the issue was already in the judicial branch, they chose not to repeal the landmark. The case appeared to end in the Second Circuit Court of Appeals (Murphy 2018). Murphy 2018 reported that the court sided with Yonkers because they believed that the ICCMW did not illustrate how the landmark status affected its capacity "to use its property, let alone . . . burdened its ability to practice its religious faith." So, the ICCMW was not successful at repealing its landmark status.

This example is helpful on several fronts. First, it illustrates the robust and diverse nature of the progressive community. Second, while they failed in their attempt to overturn the landmark status, progressives advocated on behalf of a group that appears to be discriminated against by their neighbors before their municipal government. This story, again, illustrates that there is a robust progressive presence in the Hudson Valley and in areas outside of America's largest cities. And the story illustrates how progressives use non-profits and government to fight the status quo of anti-Muslim discrimination in hope of advancing land use and religious equity and equal opportunity.

Assessment of Progressive Civic Endeavors

Progressive activists in the Hudson Valley look out for those who are often forgotten or overlooked by government elites and political parties. They engage the public directly, asking residents to articulate the policy problems that they believe are most important. In doing so, they provide a civic lifeline. Progressives also use nonprofits to provide services that government does not provide, whether helping the formally incarcerated or the impoverished. And they seek to protect those that appear to be discriminated against. Clearly, progressives are a robust and prominent part of the Hudson Valley's civic community and are found outside of America's largest cities. Thus, this work is important to understanding New York politics, and ideological engagement nationwide, beyond the Hudson River Valley. And, clearly, progressives fight the status quo by using nonprofit entities and/or governments to attempt to provide various categories of equity and equal opportunity.

Educating the Public

Progressives are civic educators. They spent a great deal of time informing others about particular policy proposals. These activists also educate people more generally about civics in a variety of ways. Indeed, they spread information.

Very broadly, Pramilla Malick told me, "I organize, mobilize. I disseminate information and I write. Those are the primary ways that I choose to affect change." Malick continued, explaining that communicating with community members is an effective way of fighting the status quo. In her efforts, she teaches others how they can achieve their desired goals and solutions. Thus, for Malick, it is not only a matter of information, but it is giving residents a civic education to become engaged in community affairs. Progressives do this in different ways.

Marjorie Hsu of Westchester was also involved in civic education. Hsu explained that the League of Women Voters approached her about creating a civic education program. Her program in 2018 focused on the midterm elections and encouraging people to vote. Her program at the time of our interview centered on the media. In particular, she gave people the tools to "discern between fact, media bias, confirmation bias, and fake news. And giving them tools for discerning facts verses fake." Other progressives provided similar tools to the public.

Dr. Maria May of Orange County recalled that the Democratic committee in her town organized a series of seminars that focused on local government. Dr. May recounted that these workshops discussed important information, like budgeting and the components of various governments. She proudly told me that most of these workshops were filled to capacity. Dr. May noted that her running mates planned another seminar on the new election rules in New York. She reflected, "So, like our whole thing is like educate people, give them the knowledge that they need to be informed." Dr. May argued that these workshops provide residents with an opportunity to feel heard, since they are able to interact with the presenters. And Dr.

May's running mates were not the only people to educate the public on voting reform.

Susan Van Dolsen of Westchester County told me that her group was in the process of hosting a forum on voting reform legislation that passed in New York. She noted that at events like this, progressive activists not only inform people about policy but work to register them to vote. They also encourage them to go to the polls and cast a ballot. Van Dolsen explained, "Last year, we had about three or four forums. What we do is we bring in a person who's an expert on the topic, whether they're in a nonprofit or in another grassroots group . . . somebody in that level of sort of academia or in a nonprofit." She stated that they invited speakers on fair elections, campaign finance reform, and easing the ability to register to vote in New York. Van Dolsen revealed that many progressive groups worked on issues, such as how to implement early voting policy, parolee enfranchisement, and working on adopting same-day voter registration. Van Dolsen explained that they educate those in attendance, and then they give them an opportunity to practice civic engagement. They show them how to become advocates. Her organization is in full agreement that before there can be advocacy, there must be education.

Lin Sakai of Ulster County told me that it is extremely important to encourage people to engage in the political process. Sakai described her attendance at an environmental rally at SUNY New Paltz. Sakai recalled that she approached a student and asked if she considered seeking public office. Lin recalled that the student appeared almost horrified and explained that she did not want to be active in the political arena. Sakai recounted that for her, this was such a "moment of awakening . . . And that's when I realized that, you know, we really have our work cut out for us, and just getting people to understand how important it is just to get their voices heard." Sakai ended by asserting that activists need to engage and inform people who are simply not content with the status quo in the hope that they become involved and inspired to become civically active. Again, education is key to this involvement.

PARTICULAR ISSUES

Progressives in the Hudson Valley work hard to create dialog on particular issues and civic endeavors and to keep people informed through various formal organizations and also, informally, through leveraging social capital.

Andrew Dalton, the treasurer of the Green Party in the region, explained that he organized a "nonpartisan meeting" on ways to move away from a reliance on property taxes to fund local schools. Dalton recalled that Democrats, Republicans, Libertarians, and Greens were present, including a town supervisor. Dalton said, "We had sort of a teach-in." Dalton recounted the conversation at the meeting included discussing why many other states do not rely on property taxes to fund public schools. They asked why New York could not move away from property taxes to fund education. Dalton observed, "I don't know how much traction we had, but we shared a lot of ideas." Other progressive activists used nonprofit organizations to engage in dialog and keep people informed.

Marjorie Hsu told me about her role as the chair of the Asian American Federation. Hsu told me that this organization is a census information center. It was explained that their research and policy director held a forum on the 2020 Census. Marjorie is interested in engaging and informing members of her group through these types of workshops. Hsu was not the only activist working to educate and inform people about the 2020 Census.

Christine Primomo of Albany County reported that she held public education seminars on the 2020 Census through her membership on the program committee of her League of Women Voters chapter. Primomo explained that the forum was held at an Albany Public Library branch, where speakers from the US Census Bureau and municipal governments, as well as nonprofits, addressed the crowd. Besides the census, progressives informed many people about immigration policy.

Dylan Basescu of Westchester introduced the issue to me, particularly safeguarding people from Immigration and Customs Enforcement. Basescu told me that there was a big drive to inform immigrants about their rights, and also to urge local police to no longer cooperate with ICE. Progressives in other parts of the Hudson Valley were also engaged with this issue. *Esther Dodson* chronicled the increased presence of ICE, especially in Rensselaer County. *Dodson* told me that there are a number of organizations in the upper Hudson Valley informing immigrants and allies about immigrant rights. *Dodson* noted, "So, if they're ever detained . . . we can do the best we can to either stop them from being detained or make sure that they're safe through the whole process." The immigration issue clearly has a criminal justice component to it. So do other issues.

Nada Khader of Westchester told me about her efforts to offer regular community forums about different issues. Soon after our initial interview,

Khader told me that her group was hosting a seminar on "the racial impact of marijuana policing in Westchester County." She noted that the forum is connected to their work on racial and criminal justice, as well as police accountability. Khader noted that marijuana usage is largely the same among white and black Americans, but marijuana arrest rates for African Americans are noticeably higher. She lamented that young people who are brought into contact with the criminal justice system through this issue are disadvantaged in pursuing education and job opportunities. Khader asserted, "And already they're negatively impacted without even having interactions with police and the criminal justice system. They're already disadvantaged in terms of employment access and education access; so, this is just compounding an existing problem." Khader proclaimed that her organization is bringing attention to this issue. Local progressive activists were also involved with women's equity.

Castina Charles, who lives in Schenectady County but articulates much of her activism in Albany and Rensselaer Counties, told me about her interest in organizing a conference. Charles continued that there were workshops and speakers at her conference, but it was important to her that admission was free. She articulated, "I wanted it to be available to anybody because I felt like sometimes there's a lot of great women's empowerment conferences . . . But sometimes it's prohibitive to certain types of people . . . And I feel like it can defeat the purpose sometimes." She noted that many of these conferences are attended by similar people and are not accessible to those outside of that group. Through Castina's efforts to raise money to hold the event for free, she founded a women's empowerment organization. And she educated women on important issues. Progressives are also involved in peace issues, particularly members of the Green Party.

Dr. Barbara Kidney, the cochair of the local Green Party, who was elected a Green Party state committee member after our interview, organized a book tour by peace activist Medea Benjamin throughout the Hudson Valley.

Dr. Kidney recalled that the purpose of the book tour focused on "drone wars," and Benjamin was in the area for two weeks. Dr. Kidney explained that she would introduce the author at every workshop and would remind attendees that when Benjamin "leaves tonight, the problem is still going to be with us, and it's going to take many people to try to solve that problem. So, if you're interested in working on that locally, sign up." Dr. Kidney recalled that she gathered contact information for eighty individuals and hoped to host "a drone café" to engage people, and hopefully some of their friends, on the issue locally. More precisely, she hopes that these cafés would lead to brainstorming strategies for stopping drones. Dr. Kidney lamented that there was not much interest in her follow-up efforts from those eighty individuals. Nevertheless, she arranged a book tour through her affiliation with Code Pink and worked to educate people on this issue.

These efforts clearly illustrate that there is a robust progressive presence in the Hudson Valley and in areas beyond America's largest cities. Further, while their plans may not always work out, progressives work diligently to inform the public about particular issues of importance. Significantly, they use their roles in nonprofit organizations to fight the status quo and provide educational equity and equal opportunity. This could lend itself to criminal justice equity and equal opportunity, in the case of marijuana and immigration. And this certainly could lead to equity and equal opportunity for their local governments, who receive funding for each and every person who fills out a census form. As such, progressives leverage nonprofits and government to achieve their goals of equity and equal opportunity.

OTHER MEANS OF EDUCATING THE PUBLIC

Progressives engage in education in a number of other ways that continue to illustrate their robust progressive presence. First, progressives show films throughout the region on a variety of issues.

Dolores Baldasare arranged an event to show a film concerning environmental issues in Rockland County. Ellen Schorsch of Greene County noted, as chair of the environmental committee of Mountain Top Progressives, that they organized the showing of free films at local libraries. Schorsch articulated, "And a lot of that is because it allows us to go into the schools and engage people in a nonpartisan way on an issue that is very important to us and should be important to them as well." Schorsch continued telling me that they are planning a movie series.

Connie Hogarth of Dutchess County explained that she hosts an event every month where attendees view a documentary. This is hosted at a local church. All of these documentaries present diverse issues that are relevant at the time of each documentary's showing. Connie told me that they take great care in their selection of films and asserted the films have been addressing things like "environmental, peace, [and] justice" issues. Then, there is often a question-and-answer period after the film with someone who knows about each particular issue. Hogarth calls this project "Movies That Matter, Beacon." She noted that activists from throughout the Hudson Valley attend these movie nights. Progressives educate people in other ways too.

In particular, progressive activists "table," as several subjects noted. At various community and public events, they sit at a table, engage the public, and disseminate information. Darrett Zephyr Roberts of Dutchess County told me that activists sit at a table with information to engage people and encourage them to become active in civic affairs, and that in order to do that, they need to present information in a way attendees find compelling: "You have to explain the story," Darrett said. He asserted that the purpose of the story is to convince people. Carolyn Guyer told me about her group's tabling program, which was very active at the time of our interview.

Guyer reported that various progressive organizations in the area often work together to make sure a table has a sufficient number of people at all times to engage the public, even if the groups have slightly different progressive focuses. Carolyn stressed the variety of events where progressive activists sit at tables to educate and engage the public. Carolyn made known that her group goes to festivals, where they sometimes bring bilingual volunteers; recreational events; farmers markets; and political party events. Besides speaking one on one to an individual at a table, progressive activists are also invited to speak publicly.

Dr. Barbara Kidney told me that she is occasionally invited to speak at Unitarian Universalist services. Dr. Kidney recounted, "And I talk about . . . walking the walk and inform people about issues including frack fuels, nuclear fuels, drones, and so on and so forth." As such, progressives educate the public in a variety of ways.

Importantly, they use nonprofits to fight the status quo and bring informational equity and equal opportunity to residents of the Hudson Valley. These stories show that there is an active progressive presence in the Hudson Valley and outside of America's largest cities.

ASSESSING PROGRESSIVE EFFORTS TO EDUCATE

Progressives inform and engage the public. That much is absolutely clear. They do so continuously and use a variety of mediums to spread awareness and information. Whether they are presenting a workshop on local government and voting reform, organizing a film series, sitting at a table at the Ulster County Fair, or speaking from the pulpit—progressive activists educate others. Their efforts clearly show that there is a robust and prominent progressive presence throughout the region and outside of America's largest cities. Further, they leveraged various nonprofit groups—Mountain Top Progressives, Code Pink, Unitarian Universalist congregations, the

League of Women Voters, among others—as means to fight the status quo of ignorance about government and policy and provide civic education equity and equal opportunity.

Symbolic Representation

Progressives in the region engage in symbolic representation. They hold rallies, marches, and vigils throughout the Hudson Valley in hopes of bringing public awareness about issues that are important to them. Importantly, these bring people together in an area.

Ginny O'Brien told me about rallies that bring attention to climate change, women's issues, and gun violence. Ginny told me that she attended a gun violence rally recently and noted her support for the Brady campaign. Ginny O'Brien reported, "So I've been involved in those kinds of movements for a while . . . I've been outraged about those things and tried to participate, financially supporting an organization, working out there protesting." Similarly, Susanne Kernan told me that there are rallies on a variety of issues in the Lower Hudson Valley.

Susanne mentioned her participation in rallies about "current events" to either oppose something she thinks is harmful or support something that she believes is beneficial. Susanne noted that she often helped to coordinate these gatherings, which became more numerous following the 2016 General Election that saw Donald Trump win the White House. Kernan noted that there were a fair number of these events before Trump's election, but they increased after that date. As an example, Susanne expressed that there have been many concerns of local residents over development issues, particularly overdevelopment. Kernan herself is worried about issues around resources, especially water. Other activists highlighted more focused issues as well.

Jacquelyn Drechsler of Rockland County told me, "Groups band together when there's a big cause . . . for this latest immigration debacle we all joined together last week for an immigration rally on the steps of the new city courthouse." Ginny O'Brien reported that progressives rallied to protest the Trump administration's immigration policies. She told me about a recent rally for Lights for Liberty in Albany. O'Brien explained that the very well attended rally, where she and her husband were participants, was organized to protest family separations at the border and ICE raids.

Dolores Baldasare told me about her work against current campaign finance policy. She not only protested *Citizens United* but also organized an action against the decision. And Dustin Reidy assisted with the organization of the Albany Women's March following the 2016 General Election. Reidy told me that several thousand people attended the Albany march. Castina Charles recounted her efforts with the Albany Women's March. "So, I went from organizing something that had about, I want to say no more than one hundred people . . . to organizing something that had a range between four thousand to seven thousand people. We did it in six weeks; we did it."

Progressives also rally over war and peace. Steven White of Rockland County explained that when he started protesting the Iraq War, his protests were met with derision. The local opposition against the war helped begin the Rockland Coalition for Peace and Justice. He called these early protests "difficult." But, White recalled, as the war progressed, he witnessed a great change in public opinion around the Iraq War. He said at protests during the latter part of the war he felt like a "rockstar standing on the corner holding up a sign that said, 'Bring the troops home now'; everybody was in favor of it now." White noted that they would protest two hours a week through the Rockland Coalition for Peace and Justice.

Beyond protesting and rallies, progressives also hold vigils. This includes peace vigils. Nick Mottern of Rockland participates in weekly antiwar vigils for Concerned Families of Westchester. Connie Hogarth of Dutchess recounted her work with Pete Seeger to organize a weekly peace vigil during the Gulf War. Hogarth noted that a peace pole was constructed at the location of the weekly vigil to commemorate these weekly gatherings. She also told me that beginning two years prior to our interview, she organized a peace rally and vigil across from the Beacon City Hall in reaction to local and national issues. Hogarth explained, "At this point it's taken on a broader scope, which is for many people, impeach Trump." And there are also environmental vigils held.

Andrew Dalton reported about a proposed crude oil pipeline that would run from Albany to Linden, New Jersey. Dalton continued, explaining that the pipeline would carry Bakken fracked crude oil, which exploded in Lac-Mégantic, Quebec. He recounted, "We actually got in touch with the people of Lac-Mégantic, when we were going to do a commemorative vigil in front of the library, and we let them know about it. They were very happy."

Progressives are no strangers to rallying, demonstrating, or holding vigils. They are engaged in a number of activities that gather like-minded individuals to make a statement, either in support of or opposition to a policy or a policy proposal. Importantly, these activities continue to demonstrate that there is a robust progressive presence in the region and that progressives are a visible part of the civic community in the Hudson Valley. Further, the stories illustrate that progressives are found outside of America's largest cities. And many of these efforts are done through various nonprofits in order to raise awareness of policy concerns, in hope of having government fight the status quo in support of equity and equal opportunity.

Conclusion

Kim Izzarelli of Westchester told me, "I do a lot of marches and rallies . . . I suppose that helps the progressive cause more than a progressive candidate." The main reason why this chapter is a stand-alone chapter is twofold. First, the items presented here do not necessarily relate to candidates and electoral politics. In other words, the actions chronicled are not part of a campaigns and elections effort, either for party positions or public offices.

Second, these actions are far more about engaging unofficial actors—groups and voters—and far less about pushing for a particular policy solution from official actors in government regarding a particular issue, such as a cement plant in Hudson, or campaign finance reform in Dutchess County, or Community Choice Aggregation in the city of Poughkeepsie. Progressives still might push government to move in broad directions in a policy area but do so in a less direct way than highlighted in the fourth chapter of this work. Obviously, all of these issues are political and have a power component, but these activities, which are certainly important, are treated separately because they are something different from the way progressives articulate their ideology as explored elsewhere in this work.

Progressives are a key part of many nonprofit initiatives that fall outside the policymaking process. These activists engage those who are normally not considered by policymakers and political parties. These activists serve as conduits, asking citizens to give their opinions about the most important issues their communities are facing. Progressives create dialog that would not happen otherwise. Their commitment to "small d" democracy is striking and heartening.

And progressives offer solutions to problems that government is not solving. They worked to help those released from prison to transition to life after incarceration. Progressives work in local communities to help with ground-up, asset-based community development. They came to the assistance of the ICCMW, even if the outcome of the situation was not their ideal.

Indeed, progressives are present, working with various communities in the Hudson Valley.

They also are key to educating the public through a variety of means, from sitting at tables, to hosting forums, to delivering sermons at UU churches, to planning movie nights. And they engage in symbolic representation—holding rallies, marches, and vigils. Indeed, they are busy.

Nevertheless, as Kim Izzarelli noted, these actions help progressive causes and the public. And these actions support the notion that there is a diverse and robust progressive presence in the Hudson Valley and outside of America's largest cities. Yes, progressives are prominent players in elections and policymaking. But they are also visible members of the civic community beyond those two realms. And through their efforts, usually leveraging nonprofits and also government, they fight the status quo in hope of providing equity and equal opportunity in different civic theaters.

The book now turns to its final chapter, which highlights progressives as coalition builders, incubators of activism, and conduits of social capital. This final chapter will also offer an assessment of lessons learned from this work.

Chapter 6

Progressives as "Incubators" of Activism

Progressives build coalitions and create social capital. In doing so, they help to create dialog within the progressive community and the Hudson Valley. Julie Goldberg noted that there is a strong progressive presence that works on a multitude of issues. She declared that progressives are largely friendly with each other and highlighted the "strength of weak ties." She disclosed that many progressives go to the same meetings and they can mobilize several hundred people because they are connected to a number of groups. This collaboration on big issues helps progressives move forward toward equity and equal opportunity. She also noted that Rockland Citizens Action Network "acts as a clearinghouse sometimes." Thus, the role of many of these nonprofit organizations is to be "incubators," as Michael Quackenbush of Dutchess County Progressive Action Alliance asserted.

Michael Quackenbush explained that DCPAA works to incubate a number of groups that operate around particular policy issues or concerns. He told me that the group is not based on a hierarchal structure, but things are run in a more parallel structure. Groups who form around an issue may continue to affiliate with DCPAA, or, they may leave the organization and continue to operate separately. Michael declared, "Just so long as they come into existence." Michael was also quick to tell me that DCPAA has a handle on its own capacity. When speaking about these action groups, he observed that DCPAA fosters the maximum number of groups that it can adequately manage at a given time. He noted that forming these groups does take effort. Part and parcel to this is ensuring that each group has the assurance that it will be able to thrive on its own. Let us look more at DCPAA and other progressive groups that build social capital.

The first part of this chapter will focus on the role of progressives as incubators and builders of social capital. As this is the last chapter of this work, it will then move forward to offer lessons learned from this study. Again, in concert with the argument, this chapter will illustrate that there is a robust progressive presence in the region, and that progressives are found outside of America's largest urban areas. Further, progressives are an important part of the electoral, policymaking, and civic arenas. Finally, progressives embrace the use of government and nonprofits to fight the status quo in hope of advancing equity and equal opportunity.

Coalitions and Social Capital

Maria Quackenbush of the Dutchess County Progressive Action Alliance told me that the group urges their action teams to connect and build partnerships with other nongovernmental organizations that share each team's positions on a given issue. Maria explained that the organization's Democracy Team formed alliances with a number of groups, including Citizen Action, Let New York Vote, and Common Cause. She also told me that the group that focuses on healthcare and the New York Health Campaign formed a partnership, as did their Sanctuary Team with the Green Light campaign. Further their Environment Team and Mothers Out Front worked together as well. As noted in the last chapter concerning a proposed power plant, groups that start with DCPAA go off on their own. Other groups concentrate their efforts solely within single counties and are also issue oriented.

Nada Khader explained, "WESPAC stands for Westchester People's Action Coalition. It's a multi-issue hub and resource center for the progressive community in Westchester County." She noted that they are known well beyond the borders of Westchester. Other organizations are more electorally focused.

Tom Denton of Ulster County talked to me about MoveOn. Tom explained that the organization urged local activists to organize meetings to combat the Trump administration. The first meeting he planned in New Paltz had over one hundred attendees, as did the second meeting he organized. Denton noted that they named their group UAct, which is short for Ulster Activists. At their first meeting, they agreed that they were not about conversing or writing, but "we're here to act." He observed that UAct is well known to local political activists and is a source of campaign volunteers, which proved beneficial on Election Day to local Democrats. Thus, Ulster

Activists is about organizing locally and appears to have a focus on electoral politics. Other groups engage in both elections and policy battles.

Rockland Citizens Action Network is an example. Gina I. noted that the group works to promote progressive policy positions and to spark civic engagement. She also noted that the genesis of their group came about through an association with the New York Progressive Action Network. Further, Rockland Citizens Action Network was a local affiliate of Rockland for Bernie. Following the 2016 Democratic National Convention, Gina remembered that activists involved in Bernie Sanders's campaign met and decided to keep their activism alive. Gina also told me that her group meets every month and discusses different topics. Further, very much like DCPAA, Gina I. told me that Rockland Citizens Action Network has "action groups" that pay attention to certain policy areas.

John Gromada explained more about Rockland Citizens Action Network. He noted that Rockland Citizens Action Network serves as a connection point for local and regional progressive groups and has helped to foster communication among the large number of activist nongovernmental organizations that came into existence following President Trump's 2016 victory. Gromada asserted that this connection hub stimulates a great deal of civic engagement among activist groups in Rockland County, New York City, and statewide nonprofits. Gromada noted that there are common issues that are of interest to each of these pockets of activists and that much of this synergy came about through leveraging social media. He professed, "And that's been incredibly powerful because we've been able to create . . . networks of people off of some similar issues and draw ideas and resources from each other across the state and New York City." Gromada stated that these networks have been extremely beneficial to all involved, particularly on issues related to the state senate. It is important to document that the committee that recruited and organized Julie Goldberg's 2018 primary campaign against Independent Democratic Conference State Senator David Carlucci were members of this organization. Rockland Citizens Action Network was established in 2016, prior to the general election. Indivisible was formed after the 2016 General Election.

Shannon Powell of Westchester compared her work with Indivisible to "a full-time job. You know, a lot of work." Powell continued, telling me that the group works to spark activism at the most local level possible. To do so, activists are generally divided by zip codes. Concerning networking and social capital, Powell asserted, "I don't even like to say we're an umbrella group. We're almost like the under-web of connecting people so they can organize. So, what we try and do is, we try and facilitate communication between groups, as best we can, keep people informed of what's going on in the county, or we try and organize events." Powell told me that Indivisible Westchester works to have their activism become realized around different types of events that activists can leverage, since hosting large events might be out of the capacity of many local groups. Becoming engaged in these large events leads to forming partnerships for Indivisible groups with other activist organizations. Powell explained that Indivisible Westchester joined a national coalition named We the People. Through this national organization, she collaborated with Planned Parenthood Action Fund, the Sierra Club, Service Employees International Union Local 32BJ, and the Communications Workers of America.

From these national efforts, Powell recalled that she hoped to form a smaller version of those coalition partners into a group in Westchester County. From there, a forum on income inequity was organized. She notes that she might not have the capacity to put on this forum, but labor does and is very interested in teaching people about this issue. Powell ended by affirming, "I really see us as being able to organize people and you know, also be a vehicle for communication and coalition building." Given that there are a number of Indivisible groups in a given area, largely because of how local the endeavor was, communication among Indivisible groups has been difficult. Indivisible Westchester has largely solved that problem, as Shannon Powell has illustrated and Craig Zumsteg confirmed. Zumsteg told me that Indivisible Westchester helps keep them all together. But other counties do not always have that luxury. So, the Democratic Party often helps to provide communication.

Carolyn M. Riggs observed that New York's nineteenth congressional district was home to about thirty Indivisible groups, but there was little organization or communication among these groups. As an example, she noted that multiple groups might show up to protest in front of an office, but they did not coordinate their efforts. Riggs noted that county Democratic committees have been acting as a communications hub for progressive activists, particularly when assembly districts overlap in different counties. Riggs told me that Democratic county chairs, in particular, keep in touch with each other for organizing purposes. Riggs continued, explaining that she was working with other county chairs at the time of our conversation to think about state senate candidates in the next election. As such, parties can also provide social capital and build coalitions, particularly across counties.

But that is not to suggest that only parties build coalitions across counties. Christine Primomo told me that close to our interview, she attended a meeting of a group called Coalition of Capital Region Progressives. This "is a group of groups" to organize progressive entities in the Capital District that includes Albany and Rensselaer Counties, among others. Other groups in the Hudson Valley build social capital around specific policy issues.

Dr. Charles Chesnavage of Westchester County explained that he works to develop partnerships as well. Chesnavage described organizations that are a part of a Hudson Valley immigration group that work for those facing deportation and on other immigrant issues. Chesnavage noted that they hosted a panel discussion on the "Muslim travel ban and immigration rights. That's an example of us trying to have some coalition building by trying to bring attention to the people that these issues have connections." Mountain Top Progressives is also working on particular issues too.

Jonathan Gross of Greene County told me about a forum on "opioid prevention and recovery" that he and Mountain Top Progressives organized. He recounted that one hundred people attended the forum that included prominent panelists. After the forum, the group hosted a Narcan training session. Gross told me that the point of this event, which was a novelty in the area, was to gain the attention of county and state agencies about the issue in Greene County. Gross reported that Mountain Top Progressives was offered a seat at the Columbia-Greene Addiction Coalition, a group of roughly twenty nonprofits. Gross told me that this forum helped create Mountain Top Advocacy Coalition, which includes roughly fifteen local activists, healthcare professionals, and business owners whose goal is to "combat the epidemic, which is huge up here—third highest overdose rate for opioid, second for heroin." While there are many successful examples of social capital and coalition building, progressives also explain that building alliances is challenging.

Carolyn Guyer recalled how important forming partnerships among groups is to her so there was not duplication of efforts among progressive groups. Guyer told me that the efforts were not easy, and she and others tried to form a coalition of progressive groups. Unfortunately, she told me that these efforts failed on more than one occasion. As such, progressive coalition building is not perfect, not always operating at peak efficiency. But progressives made strides to bring groups together and organize. Many of these coalitions became driving and visible forces in the electoral and policymaking arenas.

Yet, progressives do not need nonprofits to build social capital. Rev. Jordan Scruggs told me about an interaction with a member of the community that she had at a meeting of the Kingston Common Council concerning affordable housing. She noted that there were a large number of people who told the council that they simply do not want those in need of affordable housing in their communities. She stated that there was a person wearing a Make America Great Again hat in the chamber, and while she was speaking in defense of affordable housing, she spoke directly to him." Reverend Scruggs continued, "It was very obvious I was speaking to him and he was pissed. I mean, he was so pissed. And he like came up to me afterwards." The gentleman told Reverend Scruggs that he did not speak at all during the session, and yet she directed all of her comments directly at him. Reverend Scruggs recounted that they had a long conversation in the parking lot following the meeting, and he gave her his phone number and invited her to talk about local politics with her. She recalled how odd it was to transition from argumentative discourse to a respectful conversation. Scruggs asserted, "People need to talk to each other . . . I think that's the single most valuable thing progressives can do. And people need to talk to each other and listen to each other." But, of course, listening requires meeting. And meeting requires social interaction.

And progressives appear to be in an important position to organize within counties, across counties, and on an individual level to build coalitions and social capital. From these stories, we can see that progressives use nonprofit organizations and government to fight the status quo to advance equity and equal opportunity. This is abundantly clear by the narratives presented in this section. Finally, this clearly shows a robust progressive presence in the Hudson Valley and outside of America's largest cities.

The Place of Progressives in the Hudson Valley

Progressives are not the only force that matters in the Hudson Valley. Nor are progressives always successful in their electoral and policy pursuits. But they have, unquestionably, a robust presence in the Hudson Valley and are a visible part of the electoral, policymaking, and civic arenas. And, on the whole, they push against the status quo and advocate for policies that they believe will produce equity and equal opportunity. They work with government and the nonprofit sector to achieve their policy aims. Progressives are not simply denizens of America's largest cities, like New York, Los Angeles, or Chicago. They are found in small urban areas like Kingston, in suburban Bethlehem in Albany County, and in rural areas of Greene County.

While this work was able to analyze sixty-four interviews to illustrate a tie that binds the subjects of this work together, it is clear that progressives are not carbon copies of each other. This finding is in line with the literature reviewed in this work. Progressives are diverse in a number of ways. They hold a variety of professions. They are in college and over ninety years of age. Some have labored for over forty years, while others have been active since the November 2016 General Election. Two progressive activists were not even citizens of the United States but still advocated for policies in which they believed.

And their interests vary. Some appear to prefer to engage in electoral and party politics, arguing, as at least three different subjects noted, that policy victories are improbable without elected officials sympathetic to progressive causes. They train volunteers and candidates, recruit people to run for office, help individuals gain ballot access, connect with voters and campaign volunteers, and also run for office themselves.

Several ran because they were bothered by the actions of incumbents, such as Julie Goldberg, who started her political career in a primary election against a Democrat who kept Republicans in power. Others ran because they wanted a seat at the table, like Kamal Johnson, who was elected mayor of Hudson shortly after our interview. Each and every person who held or sought elected office in every region did so for selfless reasons: to fight the status quo in support of equity and equal opportunity. I never spoke to a subject who made me believe that they sought office for personal gain.

It is also true that progressives are not the sole reason many candidates won an election or reelection. It is equally correct to assert that progressives compose an important part of a number of successful electoral coalitions. And we should not gloss over their place in the political party apparatus. This book chronicled the activities of Democratic county committee and state committee members, Democratic town and county chairs, Working Families Party state committee members, and Green Party state committee members and county officers. And it is important to remember that county and state committee seats are chosen in primary elections.

In particular, how activists leverage New York's fusion voting rules should not be ignored. The labor that progressives go through to ensure that their preferred candidates appear on the Working Families Party ballot line is noteworthy. Both Steve Redler of Albany and David Schwartz of Westchester told poignant stories of how their work in assisting candidates to secure the

Working Families line made the difference in electoral outcomes. And, in the case of the latter, helped usher in a major policy change in the state. In other words, it is clear, progressives are an important group giving voters choices in electoral contests and their efforts matter. It is also important to note that in these efforts they seek to use government and the nonprofit political party structure as means of fighting the status quo and electing candidates that believe in equity and equal opportunity.

In the policymaking arena, progressives are active on a spectrum of issues. And their activities take two forms: working for the adoption of policy solutions to particular problems or working to stop policy proposals that they believe are damaging. And they are successful and unsuccessful at both of these tasks. They are, nevertheless, an important part of the policymaking process.

They fought environmental battles throughout the region, in some cases going back decades. From desalination plants and ash dumps, to cement plants and incinerator fuel—progressives have carried the water in defense of the environment and the people that live in the Hudson Valley. For instance, Connie Hogarth fought for the closure of Indian Point for over forty-five years. Progressives used elected and appointed offices to establish parks. Jason Angell and Dr. Maria May were among a number of individuals that worked with municipalities to give electric customers a choice to purchase renewable energy. And progressives were a part of a large coalition pressuring municipalities up and down the Hudson to declare their opposition to the Pilgrim Pipeline.

Progressives are concerned about criminal and economic justice. They helped to win Ban the Box at SUNY and worked with local law enforcement and municipalities to no longer share information with Immigration and Customs Enforcement. David Schwartz and the Westchester-Putnam Chapter of the Working Families Party were key behind-the-scenes players in a statewide minimum wage increase. Progressives adopted inclusionary zoning in Hudson and leveraged a landbank in Kingston to enhance distressed properties. Dr. Gregory Julian used his position on a school board to integrate schools. And progressives throughout the region fought for local resolutions to declare municipalities open and welcoming communities.

Sometimes they were not successful. They did not win campaign finance reform in Dutchess County, even though Caroline Fenner was able to have bipartisan legislation introduced on the matter. They were not able to stop the Greene County Jail from being built, even if they were able to work with state legislators to introduce bills that would allow Greene and Columbia Counties to share a jail. The proposed power plant opposed by DCPAA members is operating. But they clearly and unquestionably became noticeable figures in the policymaking arena.

And, in each of these instances, it was clear that they worked to move forward with policies that were supportive of equity and equal opportunity. Ensuring a clean environment is an equity and equal opportunity issue. Criminal and economic justice are equity and equal opportunity issues. Campaign finance reform is an equity and equal opportunity issue. School integration is an equity and equal opportunity issue. Even the Green Party and its opposition to drones and war are equity and equal opportunity issues. And much of this is linked to defeating the status quo to bring about policies to usher in equity and equal opportunity.

Progressives use nonprofit organizations to leverage their goals. The work of Jason Angell and the Hudson Valley Community Congress and Terence Miller and Community Voices Heard is heartening. These activists using their positions in these organizations to engage the public and listen to their needs and wants is extraordinary. Supervisor Mussmann and the efforts of Columbia County residents to establish a bail fund and Pat Strong's work with helping those released from incarceration also chronicle the work of progressive activists in working for justice. Reverend Scruggs and her involvement in asset-based community development and Dr. Charles Chesnavage and his assistance to the Islamic Community Center of Mid-Westchester continue to show the goal of progressives to fight the status quo and bring about equity and equal opportunity through government actors and nonprofits.

The role of the progressive as a civic educator in the electoral, policy-making, and civic arenas is heartily apparent. In the electoral arena, progressive activists were engaged in efforts to teach people to run for public office. They also spent countless hours training volunteers on how to campaign, especially teaching these volunteers how to canvass. And they engage and educate the public about candidates running for office, how to register to vote, and the different ways to cast ballots.

In the policymaking arena, they also educate different groups. First, they clearly work to educate policymakers and do so in a variety of ways. One important point that should not be missed is that many of these activists have direct access to elected officials. Access to policymakers yields significant power. And many progressives have that power and use it to educate these policymakers.

Marjorie Hsu of Westchester spoke about her connection with County Executive George Latimer. She told me they were exchanging emails the day before our interview and that she felt heartened to build a strong relationship with a local official.

They also use their roles as elected officials to educate other policymakers. Supervisor Linda Mussmann explained, "Women supervisors, I'm in the minority of the minority of the minority. So, being in the room is my job. If I have a job, or if I make a change, it's being in the room. And what being in the room means is it creates a certain zone of uncomfortable. It's not business as usual. It's like, oh, there's a lesbian in the room; you better be careful." Supervisor Mussmann continued, telling me that she asks questions to slow policy down so proposals can be considered more thoroughly. Thus, this access, either through a formally elected position, or none at all, continues to illustrate their role as civic educators.

Progressives also educate the public. They hold meetings and forums, produce and distribute literature, and write and maintain social media and websites. Their robust use of symbolic representation in rallies, protests, and marches brings awareness about issues to the public's attention.

And progressives educate themselves. It is hard to imagine that progressives who use nonprofits to listen to the needs of people, or choose to live in the communities that they work in, are not educated about the needs of citizens from different backgrounds. Progressives create coalitions and dialog. They work together. They are incubators of activism in the policy arena, in the electoral arena, and in the community at large. And they create social capital and civic learning in this process.

That does not mean that they always agree with each other. This does not suggest that they always support the same candidates in a primary, or in the case of the Green Party in particular, in a general election. It does not mean that they always like each other. It does not mean that they always coordinate effectively. But it does mean that they are a robust source of social capital.

And all of this supports the central premises of this work. First, there is a robust progressive presence in the Hudson Valley. Indeed, progressives are a visible and important part of the electoral, policymaking, and civic arenas. Second, there is a robust progressive presence outside of America's largest cities. And third, progressives use government and nonprofit entities to fight the status quo to work to bring about equity and equal opportunity. The preceding pages make that much plain.

A Progressive Movement?

There is certainly an ideological predilection that binds the subjects in this work together. Indeed, as stated numerous times, they fight against the status quo in order to usher in policies that they hope produce equity and equal opportunity. That is clear. But to say that there is a unified movement would be an overreach.

First, the Green Party activists, generally, do not support candidates endorsed by the Democratic and Working Families Parties. Second, there is not always unity among subjects going into an election, even if they are members of the same party. Indeed, on at least one occasion, Mountain Top Progressives and the Greene County Democratic Committee endorsed different candidates in a general election.

Additionally, a number of subjects are rather clear that they do not believe that every person who calls themselves progressive is a progressive. One subject considers herself a socialist. Another differentiates by adopting the term *principled progressive*. And not everyone had kind things to say about Indivisible, whom many believe is just too moderate, in comparison to groups like Lower Hudson Valley Progressive Action Network. A handful of subjects criticized the Working Families Party for not being truly progressive.

Further, the number of congressional and state legislative districts in the area also work to both divide and unite activists in different parts of the Hudson Valley. On the one hand, there are different congressional districts, and, in particular, competitive state senate districts. And progressives often choose to concentrate on their own races. Yet, the sprawling and competitive nature of the nineteenth congressional district often brings activists together from inside and outside the actual district.

Given the number of counties and municipalities below a county level, many activists concentrate on efforts in their own backyards. As Lin Sakai notes, these activists move from one election cycle to another, without a break.

Further, while there are a great many efforts to work together, and some counties do so more efficiently than others, marshaling progressives over ten counties into a single unified force is a tall order. Indeed, it is fair to say that there are progressive activists throughout the Hudson Valley who organize and are a visible part of the electoral, policymaking, and civic arenas. It is quite another to suggest, given the size of the region, the number of municipalities present, and the way legislative districts are drawn that there is a single, unified progressive movement.

Nevertheless, there is a robust progressive presence in the Hudson Valley, and progressives engage in civic activities in other places beside America's largest cities. This second argument is important. Too often media highlight the urban-rural partisan divide. Indeed, we know that many rural areas vote reliably Republican and many urban areas vote consistently Democratic. But this is not the entire case. First, the work illustrates that there is a robust presence of left-wing activists in rural areas. And the Hudson Valley is not the only rural area with a robust progressive presence. Indeed, look at many counties in the state of Vermont or Bayfield County, Wisconsin. The opposite is also true, as New York City does have Republican activists in many densely populated areas like Southern Brooklyn, the Upper East Side of Manhattan, and Northeast Queens. And look at Tarrant County in Texas, home of Fort Worth, which has a history of voting Republican but has been highly competitive recently for both parties. It is very tidy to assume that there is a clear delineation between urban and rural areas, and how they vote. This work highlights that a more nuanced approach to geographic political assumptions is in order.

This point should not be overstated. Clearly Hamilton County, New York and Susquehanna County, Pennsylvania are likely not voting Democratic in a presidential election in the near future. But it should also not be assumed that every voter in Hamilton or Susquehanna Counties are conservative Republicans. Democrats can exist in rural areas, and articulate their civic engagement robustly, just as Republicans and conservatives can be found in what are generally considered the most liberal areas of the nation like Madison, Wisconsin.

As such, with a healthy dose of qualification given the intricacies of New York State's political structure, this work should help scholars and students think about ideological and partisan activism in different parts of the nation.

Real Politics Meets Real Social Science

A few years ago, a political scientist at another institution discovered that I was working on this project. To paraphrase, he expressed that it looked as though my research talks about actual politics and observed that studying actual politics is a rarity in political science.

This book is meant to use social science as a tool to teach students of New York and students of politics real, on-the-ground politics as it happened in one electorally competitive region of the United States that happens to not be inside one of America's largest cities. This is why the words and stories of activists appear so prominently in this work. These are the people who engage in real politics. The subjects who took the time to tell me their stories deserve to have them conveyed. The reader also should hear their narratives.

Their words chronicle how citizens engage in the electoral, policy-making, and civic arenas. These activists are a key part of ensuring that the Democrats hold supermajorities in the state assembly and state senate. And, as of this writing, these activists are a key factor that could derail the Republican majority in the US House of Representatives. Indeed, at the time of this writing, if every Republican representing the Hudson Valley in Congress lost their congressional seats, which they initially won by very small margins, along with a few more Republican US representatives from Long Island—power dynamics in the US House of Representatives could change dramatically.

Beyond that, and perhaps more importantly, progressives offer citizens choices in electoral contests, both in the primary and general elections, and do the work needed to have party nominees elected to public office.

The stories here are real accounts of progressive involvement in the electoral process, policymaking arena, and civic community. And progressives are a robust and diverse part of each of these realms. In other words, these activists articulate their participation in an electorally competitive region, rich with theaters to manufacture policy and opportunities to practice civic engagement. This does not mean that there is not a robust conservative presence in the region. But it does mean that civic life is alive and well in the Hudson Valley, and progressives, in the twenty-first-century manifestation of Tocqueville's "nation of joiners," are a prominent and important part of the civic and political mosaic of New York's magnificent Hudson Valley and in areas outside of our largest cities. And, just as importantly, beyond their visible presence, the subjects reveal that they fight the status quo in the hope of advancing equity and equal opportunity.

Appendixes

Appendix A. Subjects Interviewed

Following is a list of subjects who chose to be identified in this work, along with any affiliations they wished to have put into the record. All affiliations reported were current at the time of the interview. Affiliations do not suggest that these subjects speak on behalf of the groups with which they identify. Subjects who wished to not have their names identified were given pseudonyms that appear in italics. Any similarity in pseudonym names, living or deceased, is purely coincidental.

Jason K. Angell—Longhaul Farm, Ecological Citizen's Project.

Dolores Baldasare—Rockland Coalition to End the New Jim Crow—Member; Move 9—Member.

Dylan Basescu—Democrat, Indivisible Westchester—Member; George Washington University College Democrats—Member.

Kat Brezler—Public School Teacher; People for Bernie Sanders—Cofounder.

Castina Charles—Women's Empowerment Conference and March—Cofounder.

Charles S. Chesnavage, PhD—Westchester Coalition Against Islamophobia—President.

Andrew W. Dalton—Hudson Valley Green Party—Treasurer; New Paltz Climate Action Coalition—Member; American Psychological Association Division 48, Peace Psychology—Member.

Émilia Decaudin—Yorktown Democratic Committee—Member; Westchester County Democratic Committee—Member; Lower Hudson Valley Progressive Action Network—Founding Member and Executive Committee; New York Progressive Action Network—Founding Member and Executive

Committee; New York State Democratic Committee—Candidate; City College Democrats—Founder and President.

Tom Denton—Ulster Activists (UAct)—Member.

Jacquelyn Drechsler.

Andrew Falk—Working Families Party State Committee—Member.

Caroline Fenner—Dutchess County Progressive Action Alliance—Member.

Jen Fuentes—Esopus Democratic Committee—Member; Ulster County Democratic Committee—Member.

Julie Goldberg.

Steven Greenfield.

Anthony Grice—Democratic Party; Working Families Party; Community Voices Heard; Alpha Phi Alpha, Inc.; NAACP; Local Progress.

John Gromada—Rockland Citizens Action Network—Vice President.

Jonathan Gross—Democrat; Mountain Top Progressives—Member; Greene County Board of Ethics—Chairman.

Carolyn Guyer—ACT 18 Indivisible.

Connie Hogarth—Connie Hogarth Center for Social Action at Manhattanville College—Director.

Marjorie Hsu—Indivisible 10591—Coleader; Indivisible Rivertowns—Coleader; League of Women Voters—Director; Asian American Federation—Civics Chair; Sleepy Hollow Planning Board—Chair.

Gina I.—Rockland Citizens Action Network, Orangetown Democratic Committee—Member; Rockland for Bernie (2015–2016).

Kim Izzarelli.

Kamal Johnson—City of Hudson First Ward Alderman.

Gregory B. Julian, PhD

Dean Kernan.

Susanne P. Kernan—Rockland CAN—President.

Nada Khader—WESPAC Foundation, Inc.—Executive Director; Progressive Utilization Theory, North America Chapter—Steering Committee Member.

Barbara A. Kidney, PhD—Hudson Valley Green Party—Cochair; Drone Alert Hudson Valley—Founding Member (2013–2015); American Psychological Association Division 48, Society for the Study of Peace, Conflict, and Violence—Member.

Alan Levin—Network of Holistic Activists.

Mark A. Lieberman—Indivisible Yorktown, New York—Cochair; Yorktown Democratic Committee—District Leader.

Dr. Ron Lipton.

Pramilla Malick—Protect Orange County, Chair; NYPAN, Founding Board Member; Stop MCS, Founder; Principled Progressives of Orange County, Founder.

Dr. Maria May—New York Democratic Party, Tuxedo Democratic Committee—Member. Indivisible Hudson Valley.

Terence Miller—Yonkers Democratic Committee—District Leader; Community Voices Heard—Member.

Nick Mottern—Knowdrones.com—Coordinator; WESPAC Foundation—Member; Concerned Families of Westchester.

Linda Mussmann—Columbia County—Supervisor, Fourth Ward Hudson; Columbia County Bail Fund—President and Founder; Hudson City Democrats—Former Chair; Time and Space Limited Theater Company, Hudson, New York—Founder and Director; Dewitt-Clinton Award for Community Service—Recipient.

Ginny O'Brien—Democrat.

Shannon Powell—Indivisible Westchester—Cofounder.

Christine Primomo, RN—League of Women Voters of Albany County; Coeymans Democratic Committee—Member.

Maria Quackenbush—Dutchess County Progressive Action Alliance—Cofounder.

Michael Quackenbush—Dutchess County Progressive Action Alliance (Nonpartisan, Issues-Based)—Cofounder.

Steve Redler.

Dustin Michael Reidy—NY19 Votes—Founder; Indivisible NY19.

London Reyes—Yonkers Democratic Committee—District Leader, Ward 2, Election District 26; Lower Hudson Valley Progressive Action Network—Cofounder; AAA All-Stars, a 501(c) 3 not-for-profit organization—Executive Director.

Carolyn M. Riggs—Democrat, Greene County Democratic Committee—Chair; Rural Majority Project—Cofounder, Campaign Manager and Consultant.

Darrett Zephyr Roberts—Dutchess County Progressive Action Alliance—Member; End the New Jim Crow Action Network—Member.

Lin Sakai—Esopus Democratic Committee—Member; Ulster County Democratic Committee—Member; Indivisible NY19; Hudson Valley Progressives.

Ellen Schorsch—Mountain Top Progressives.

David Schwartz—Westchester-Putnam Chapter of the Working Families Party—Vice Chair.

John Schwartz—Town of Rosendale Democratic Committee—Chair.
Rev. Jordan Scruggs—United Methodist Church, New York Annual Conference.
Pat Courtney Strong—Courtney-Strong, Inc.
Susan Van Dolsen—Westchester for Change—Cofounder; Stop the Algonquin Pipeline Expansion—Cofounder.
Steven White—*Power of Ten*—Publisher; Rockland County Democratic Committee—Member; Rockland Citizens Action Coalition—Steering Committee; Rockland County Civil Rights Hall of Fame—Inductee.
Tasha Young—Westchester Women's Agenda.
Andrew Zink—Ulster County Democratic Committee—Treasurer.
Craig Zumsteg—NY19 Votes

Appendix B. Progressives on the Hudson: Their Impact on Politics and Policymaking

INTERVIEW QUESTIONS

Since this is a qualitative analysis, it is customary to ask open-ended questions of each subject in hope of understanding the contours of progressive political ideology and activism in the Hudson Valley.

Overall Questions About the Activist:

Please tell me about *how* you are politically active.
Please tell me about *why* you are politically active.
Please tell me why you consider yourself to be a progressive.
What does being a progressive mean to you?
How do you define the term *progressive*?

Overall Questions About Progressives in the Hudson Valley:

Please tell me about progressive politics and activists in your county or in the Hudson Valley. What is the progressive movement's composition? What is it trying to accomplish in terms of politics and policy? Is there a strong progressive presence? If so, how or why?
What are the policy successes and failures of progressives in your county or in the Hudson Valley?

What are the political successes and failures of progressives in your county or in the Hudson Valley?

Political Party Involvement:

Please tell me about any *political parties* that you are involved with—either as a party official or in a party club—and what you do for that party.

Are you enrolled in this party? If so, why? If not, what party are you enrolled in and why?

If you hold an elected political party office, why did you run for that position? Also, were you, or have you ever been elected to that position in a contested primary election?

Nongovernmental Organization Involvement:

Please tell me about any progressive *nongovernmental organizations* (beyond parties) that you are involved with—and what you do for those organizations.

Has this organization been successful in advancing its goals? If so, how? If not, why not?

Policy:

What policy issues are most important to you? Why is this the case?

What policies have you successfully been involved in getting adopted, are currently fighting for, or would like to see become law? How have you engaged in policy activism?

For Elected Public Officials:

If you are an elected public official, why did you run for office?

If you are an elected public official, please tell me about your campaigns and your public activities.

For Unsuccessful Candidates for Public Office:

What offices did you seek and why did you run for office?

Please tell me about your campaigns.

Supporting Progressive Candidates:

Please tell me about some of the progressive candidates for public offices or party positions that you supported. And, then, please tell me how you were involved in their campaigns.

Your Progressive Successes:

Tell me about your successes in the realm of progressive politics and policymaking.

Your Progressive Vision:

What is your progressive vision for the Hudson Valley, New York State, and the United States?

Anything Else?

Since this is a qualitative analysis, is there any other relevant information related to your involvement in progressive politics and policymaking that may be important to the project?

References

American Presidency Project. "1924 Presidential Election." Accessed June 24, 2017. http://www.presidency.ucsb.edu/showelection.php?year=1924.

Armato, Michael A. 2022. "'The One Who Spells It with a Capital L': Liberal Party Activism in the Hudson River Valley, 1948–1963." *Hudson River Valley Review* 38 (2): 44–62.

Barry, John W. 2017. "Poughkeepsie Declares Itself 'Safe City' for Undocumented Immigrants." *Poughkeepsie Journal*, June 20, 2017. https://www.poughkeepsiejournal.com/story/news/2017/06/20/poughkeepsie-safe-city-immigrants/412596001/.

Bell, Jonathan, and Timothy Stanley, eds. 2012. *Making Sense of American Liberalism*. Urbana: University of Illinois Press.

Benjamin, Gerald. 1974. "Patterns in New York State Politics." *Proceedings of the Academy of Political Science* 31, no. 3 (May): 31–44.

Benjamin, Gerald. 2017. "The Chassidic Presence and Local Government in the Hudson Valley." *Albany Law Review* 80 (4): 1383–1464.

Biographical Directory of the United States Congress. "La Follette, Robert Marion." Accessed June 24, 2017. http://bioguide.congress.gov/scripts/biodisplay.pl?index=l000004.

Brennen Center for Justice. 2002. "Westchester County (New York) Passes Living Wage Law." Accessed December 12, 2021. https://www.brennancenter.org/our-work/analysis-opinion/westchester-county-new-york-passes-living-wage-law.

City of Kingston. 2020. "City of Kingston and Kingston City Landbank Announce First Acquisitions." Accessed December 12, 2021. https://www.kingston-ny.gov/news/?FeedID=1224.

Clark, Peter B., and James Q. Wilson. 1961. "Incentive Systems: A Theory of Organizations." *Administrative Science Quarterly* 6 (2): 129–166.

Climate Smart Communities. n.d. "Why Become Certified." Accessed December 11, 2021. https://climatesmart.ny.gov/actions-certification/why-become-certified/.

Clucas, Richard A., Mark Henkels, and Brent S. Steel, eds. 2005. *Oregon Politics and Government: Progressives versus Conservative Populists*. Lincoln: University of Nebraska Press.

Coalition Against Pilgrim Pipeline. n.d. "Pilgrims Proposed Pipelines." Accessed December 11, 2021. https://stoppilgrimpipeline.com/.

Coalition Against Pilgrim Pipeline. n.d.a. "Resolutions and Ordinances." Accessed December 11, 2021. https://stoppilgrimpipeline.com/resolutions/.

Columbia County Bail Fund. 2019. "The Columbia County Bail Fund Is Not Accepting Donations at This Time, but We Encourage Our Supporters to Donate to Their Choice of One of These Other Incredible Community Bail Funds Operating Around the Country, in Honor of #freethepeopleday!" Facebook, December 31, 2019. https://www.facebook.com/columbiacountybailfund.

Columbia County Bail Fund. 2020. "Bail Reform: Please Read." Facebook, January 1, 2020. https://www.facebook.com/columbiacountybailfund.

Columbia County Board of Elections. 2017. "GE 17 Results." Accessed December 10, 2021. https://sites.google.com/a/columbiacountyny.com/elections/election-information/election-results/2017-election-cycle/ge17-results?authuser=0.

Cook Political. 2023. "2023 Cook PVISM: District Map and List (118th Congress)." Accessed April 26, 2023. https://www.cookpolitical.com/cook-pvi/2023-partisan-voting-index/118-district-map-and-list.

Cramer, Katherine J. 2016. *The Politics of Resentment: Rural Consciousness in Wisconsin and the Rise of Scott Walker.* Chicago: University of Chicago Press.

Cruz, José E. 1998. *Identity and Power: Puerto Rican Politics and the Challenge of Ethnicity.* Philadelphia, PA: Temple University Press.

Daily Freeman. 2017. "Ulster County Comptroller Auerbach Endorsed for Re-election by Working Families Party." *Daily Freeman,* June 19, 2017. http://www.dailyfreeman.com/general-news/20170619/ulster-county-comptroller-auerbach-endorsed-for-re-election-by-working-families-party.

DeLeon, Richard Edward. 1992. *Left Coast City: Progressive Politics in San Francisco, 1975–1991.* Topeka: University Press of Kansas.

Duncan, James S., and Nancy G. Duncan. 2004. *Landscapes of Privilege: The Politics of the Aesthetic in an American Suburb.* London: Routledge.

Dunne, Allison. 2017. "Hudson City Council Passes Sanctuary City Resolution." WAMC, March 22, 2017. https://www.wamc.org/hudson-valley-news/2017-03-22/hudson-city-council-passes-sanctuary-city-resolution.

Dutchess County Progressive Action Alliance. 2021. "DCPAA Action Teams." Accessed December 19, 2021. https://www.dcpaa.org/dcpaa-action-teams/.

Ecological Citizens. n.d. "People-Centered Democracy." Accessed December 14, 2021. http://ecologicalcitizens.org/peoplecentereddemocracy.

Eisner, J. M. 1969. "Politics, Legislation, and the ILGWU." *American Journal of Economics and Sociology* 28, no. 3 (July): 301–314.

Fego, Emily. 2020. "New Albany County Clean Air Act Considered Toughest in the State." *Legislative Gazette,* September 20, 2020. https://legislativegazette.com/new-albany-county-clean-air-act-considered-toughest-in-the-state/.

Fenno, Richard F. 1978. *Home Style: House Members in Their Districts.* New York: Longman.

Fenno, Richard F. 2013. *The Challenge of Congressional Representation.* Cambridge, MA: Harvard University Press.

Fisher, Dana. 2006. *Activism, Inc.: How the Outsourcing of Grassroots Campaigns Is Strangling Progressive Politics in America.* Stanford, CA: Stanford University Press.

Flad, Harvey K., and Clyde Griffen. 2009. *Main Street to Mainframes: Landscape and Social Change in Poughkeepsie.* Albany: State University of New York Press.

Friedman, Sally. 2007. *Dilemmas of Representation: Local Politics, National Factors, and the Home Styles of Modern U.S. Congress Members.* Albany: State University of New York Press.

Fuller, Wayne E. 1968. "The Rural Roots of the Progressive Leaders." *Agricultural History* 42 (1): 1–14.

Gendron, Richard, and G. William Domhoff. 2009. *The Leftmost City: Power and Progressive Politics in Santa Cruz.* Boulder, CO: Westview Press.

Green, Bruce A., and Rebecca Roiphe. 2020. "When Progressive Prosecutors Politick: Progressive Law Enforcers Then and Now." *Journal of Criminal Law and Criminology* 110 (4): 719–768.

Green Party of New York State. 2015. "Rules of the Green Party of New York State." Accessed June 1, 2017. http://www.gpny.org/gpny_rules.

Greenberg, Stanley B., and Theda Skocpol, eds. 1997. *The New Majority: Toward a Popular Progressive Politics.* New Haven, CT: Yale University Press.

Greene County, New York. 2019. "Greene County Jail Facility Bond Sale, Favorable Interest Rates and Investor Confidence." Accessed December 14, 2021. https://www.greenegovernment.com/scoop/greene-county-jail-facility-bond-sale-favorable-interest-rates-and-investor-confidence.

Gunnell, John G. 2001. "The Archaeology of American Liberalism." *Journal of Political Ideologies* 6 (2): 125–145.

Hallisay, Michael. 2020. "Coeymans Declaws Clean Air Law." *Spotlight News,* December 2, 2020. https://spotlightnews.com/news/2020/12/02/coeymans-declaws-clean-air-law/.

Hannigan Gilson, Roger. 2021. "Hudson's Common Council Passes Groundbreaking Anti-Eviction Law." *Times Union,* September 22, 2021. https://www.timesunion.com/hudsonvalley/news/article/Hudson-s-Common-Council-passes-groundbreaking-16479656.php.

Hart, Gary. 1997. "The Mysterious Disappearance of American Liberalism." *Journal of Political Ideologies* 2 (3): 227–238.

Hudson River Valley Institute. "The Hudson River Valley." Accessed June 6, 2017. http://www.hudsonrivervalley.org/.

Indivisible. n.d. "Find Your Local Group." Accessed December 18, 2021. https://indivisible.org/groups.

Indivisible. n.d.a. "About." Accessed December 18, 2021. https://indivisible.org/about.

Internal Revenue Service. 2021. "Exempt Organization Types." Accessed December 30, 2021. https://www.irs.gov/charities-non-profits/exempt-organization-types.

Jackson, Colleen R. 2021. "The Vermont Difference: Direct Democracy to the Impact of Progressive Politics." Master's thesis. Johns Hopkins University.

Jaschik, Scott. 2016. "SUNY Bans the Box." *Inside Higher Education*, September 15, 2016. https://www.insidehighered.com/news/2016/09/15/suny-removes-question-criminal-convictions-application.

Joule Community Power. 2021. "Hudson Valley Community Power." Accessed December 11, 2021. https://www.hudsonvalleycommunitypower.com/.

Karlin, Rick. 2019. "Rensselaer County Lawmakers Pass Moratorium on Solid Waste Facilities." *Albany Times Union*, July 10, 2019. https://www.timesunion.com/news/article/Rensselaer-county-lawmakers-look-to-solid-waste-14085990.php.

Kemble, William J. 2015. "Rosendale Ranked Third Most Liberal Community in U.S." *Daily Freeman*, December 21, 2015. http://www.dailyfreeman.com/article/DF/20151221/NEWS/151229958.

Kemble, William J. 2017. " 'Sanctuary City': Kingston Council Adopts Resolution Declaring City 'Welcoming and Inclusive' to Immigrants. *Daily Freeman*, January 11, 2017. https://www.dailyfreeman.com/2017/01/11/sanctuary-city-kingston-council-adopts-resolution-declaring-city-welcoming-and-inclusive-to-immigrants/.

Kerbel, Matthew Robert. 2009. *Netroots Online Progressives and the Transformation of American Politics*. Boulder, CO: Paradigm.

Khader, Nada. 2013. "About WESPAC." Accessed December 18, 2021. https://wespac.org/2013/06/11/about-wespac/.

Kingston City Landbank. 2024. "By-laws of the Kingston City Landbank, Inc." Accessed January 18, 2025. https://kclb.org/wp-content/uploads/2024/03/KCLB-By-Laws-032524-FINAL-CLEAN.pdf

Kneeland, Timothy W. 2021. *Declaring Disaster: Buffalo's Blizzard of '77 and the Creation of FEMA*. Syracuse, NY: Syracuse University Press.

Kramer, Daniel C., and Richard M. Flanagan. 2012. *Staten Island: Conservative Bastion in a Liberal City*. Lanham, MD: University Press of America.

Kraus, Neil. 2000. *Race, Neighborhoods, and Community Power: Buffalo Politics, 1934–1997*. Albany: State University of New York Press.

Levine, Peter. 2000. *The New Progressive Era: Toward a Fair and Deliberative Democracy*. New York: Rowman & Littlefield.

Liberal Party Records. 1956. Unnamed Press Release, 20 June 1956, box. 99, f. Putnam Valley—Decision of Appellate Division on Voters, Liberal Party of New York State Records 1936–2002. New York Public Library.

Liberal Party Records. 1956a. Unnamed Press Release, 5 July 1956, box. 99, f. Putnam County on Reversal of Javits Decision, Liberal Party of New York State Records 1936–2002. New York Public Library.

Lifset, Robert D. 2014. *Power on the Hudson: Storm King Mountain and the Emergence of Modern American Environmentalism*. Pittsburgh: University of Pittsburgh Press.

Lucas, Dave. 2017. "Albany Mayor's Executive Order Restates Police Policy on Immigration Status." WAMC, April 25, 2017. https://www.wamc.org/capital-region-news/2017-04-25/albany-mayors-executive-order-restates-police-policy-on-immigration-status.

Lueck, Thomas J. 2004. "Police Charge New Paltz Mayor for Marrying Same-Sex Couples." *New York Times*, March 3, 2004. http://www.nytimes.com/2004/03/03/nyregion/police-charge-new-paltz-mayor-for-marrying-same-sex-couples.html?mcubz=2&_r=0.

Lungariello, Mark. 2018. "Westchester Blocks Questions About Conviction History on Job Applications." Accessed December 12, 2021. https://www.lohud.com/story/news/local/westchester/2018/12/03/westchester-county-conviction-info-ban-box/2037816002/.

McCann, Michael. 1996. "Causal versus Constitutive Explanations (or, On the Difficulty of Being So Positive . . .)." *Law and Social Inquiry* 21 (2): 457–482.

McCoy-McKay, Janette A. 2021. "'Remember the Ladies' in the 'Secret Garden': Perceptions of Female Local Political Committee Members on the Recruitment of Female Candidates for Local Elected Office—A Descriptive Phenomenological Study." PhD dissertation, St. John Fisher University.

McCright, Aaron M., and Riley E. Dunlap. 2008. "The Nature and Social Bases of Progressive Social Movement Ideology: Examining Public Opinion Toward Social Movements." *Sociological Quarterly* 49 (4): 825–848.

McKenna, Chris. 2019. "Tuxedo Residents Overwhelmingly Support New Village." *Times Herald Record*, July 17, 2019. https://www.recordonline.com/story/news/2019/07/17/tuxedo-voters-overwhelmingly-supported-new/4674162007/.

MidHudson News. 2017. "May Day Rally Calls for Poughkeepsie to Become a 'Sanctuary City,' and Keep Its Buses." *MidHudson News*, May 2, 2017. https://www.midhudsonnews.com/News/2017/May/02/Pok_sanc_city_CVH_rally-02May17.html.

Mollenkopf, John H. 1994. *A Phoenix in the Ashes: The Rise and Fall of the Koch Coalition in New York City Politics*. Princeton, NJ: Princeton University Press.

Murphy, Dan. 2018. "Yonkers Mosque Loses Appeal." *Yonkers Times*, July 21, 2018. https://yonkerstimes.com/yonkers-mosque-loses-appeal/.

Muscavage, Nick. 2016. "Sanders' Supporters See Opening in Clinton's Home State." *Poughkeepsie Journal*, February 4, 2016. http://www.poughkeepsiejournal.com/story/news/local/new-york/2016/02/04/sanders-supporters-see-opening-clintons-home-state/79833784/.

Nahmias, Laura. 2014. "After Bruising Floor Fight, Cuomo Wins W.F.P. Nomination." *Politico*, May 31, 2014. https://www.politico.com/states/new-york/albany/story/2014/05/after-bruising-floor-fight-cuomo-wins-wfp-nomination-013321.

New York Department of Labor. 2016. "New York's Largest Private Sector Employers." Accessed June 24, 2017. https://www.labor.ny.gov/stats/nys/Largest-private-sector-employers-NYS.shtm.

New York Department of State. n.d. "State Environmental Quality Review Act (SEQRA) Basics." Accessed December 13, 2021. https://dos.ny.gov/state-environmental-quality-review-act-seqra-basics.

New York Department of State, n.d.a. "State Coastal Management Program." Accessed December 13, 2021. https://dos.ny.gov/state-coastal-management-program.

New York Department of State. 2015. "New York State Constitution." Accessed June 24, 2017. https://www.dos.ny.gov/info/pdfs/Constitution%20January%20 2015%20amd.pdf.

New York Immigrant Coalition. 2018. "Signed, Sealed, Delivered! Westchester County Executive Latimer Delivers Immigrant Protection Act." Accessed December 12, 2021. https://www.nyic.org/2018/03/signed-sealed-delivered-westchester-county-executive-latimer-delivers-immigrant-protection-act/.

New York State Assembly. 2019. "A07968A." Accessed December 14, 2021. https:// nyassembly.gov/leg/?default_fld=&leg_video=&bn=A07968&term=2019&-Summary=Y&Actions=Y&Committee%26nbspVotes=Y&Floor%26nbsp Votes=Y&Memo=Y&Text=Y&LFIN=Y.

New York State Assembly. 2019a. "S06267A." Accessed December 14, 2021. https:// nyassembly.gov/leg/?default_fld=&leg_video=&bn=S06267&term=2019& Summary=Y&Actions=Y&Committee%26nbspVotes=Y&Floor%26nbsp-Votes=Y.

New York State Board of Elections. 2002. "Total Statewide Enrollment." Accessed May 1, 2017. http://www.elections.ny.gov/NYSBOE/enrollment/county/ county_jun02.pdf.

New York State Board of Elections. 2004. "NYS Board of Elections Senate Vote—Nov. 2, 2004." Accessed December 12, 2021. https://www.elections.ny.gov/NYSBOE/ elections/2004/2004nyssenate.pdf.

New York State Board of Elections. 2012. "2012 Election Results." Accessed December 9, 2021. https://www.elections.ny.gov/2012ElectionResults.html.

New York State Board of Elections. 2014. "NYS Board of Elections Assembly Election Returns November 4, 2014." Accessed May 1, 2017. https://www.elections. ny.gov/NYSBOE/elections/2014/general/2014Assembly.pdf.

New York State Board of Elections. 2014a. "NYS Board of Elections Governor/Lt. Governor Election Returns November 4, 2014." Accessed May 1, 2017. https:// www.elections.ny.gov/NYSBOE/elections/2014/general/2014Governor.pdf.

New York State Board of Elections. 2014b. "NYS Board of Elections Senate Election Returns November 4, 2014." Accessed May 1, 2017. https://www.elections. ny.gov/NYSBOE/elections/2014/general/2014Senate.pdf.

New York State Board of Elections. 2014c. "Statewide Democratic Gubernatorial Primary." Accessed May 1, 2017. https://www.elections.ny.gov/NYSBOE/ elections/2014/Primary/2014StateLocalPrimaryElectionResults.pdf.

New York State Board of Elections. 2016. "Democratic Presidential Primary by County April 19, 2016." Accessed May 1, 2017. https://www.elections.ny.gov/NYSBOE/elections/2016/Primary/DemocraticPresPrimaryResults.pdf.

New York State Board of Elections. 2016a. "NYS Board of Elections Assembly Election Returns Nov. 8, 2016." Accessed May 1, 2017. https://www.elections.ny.gov/NYSBOE/elections/2016/General/2016Assembly.pdf.

New York State Board of Elections. 2016b. "NYS Board of Elections Senate Election Returns Nov. 8, 2016." Accessed May 1, 2017. https://www.elections.ny.gov/NYSBOE/elections/2016/General/2016Senate.pdf.

New York State Board of Elections. 2017. "Running for Office." Accessed December 1, 2017. https://www.elections.ny.gov/RunningOffice.html.

New York State Board of Elections. 2018. "2018 Election Results." Accessed December 8, 2021. https://www.elections.ny.gov/2018ElectionResults.html.

New York State Board of Elections. 2020. "2020 Election Results." Accessed December 22, 2021. https://www.elections.ny.gov/2020ElectionResults.html.

New York State Board of Elections. 2021. "State of New York Election Law." Accessed December 2, 2021. https://www.elections.ny.gov/NYSBOE/download/law/2021ElectionLaw.pdf.

New York State Board of Elections. 2021a. "Committee Types." Accessed December 2, 2021. https://www.elections.ny.gov/CFCommittees.html.

New York State Energy Research and Development Authority. 2021. "Community Choice Aggregation." Accessed December 11, 2021. https://www.nyserda.ny.gov/All-Programs/Clean-Energy-Communities/How-It-Works/Toolkits/Community-Choice-Aggregation.

New York State Legislative Task Force on Demographic Research and Reapportionment. 2012. "View District Maps." Accessed June 24, 2017. http://www.latfor.state.ny.us/maps/.

New York Times. 2016. "New York Results." Accessed May 1, 2017. https://www.nytimes.com/elections/results/new-york.

New York Times. 2016a. "New York Primary Results." *New York Times.* Accessed May 1, 2017. https://www.nytimes.com/elections/2016/results/primaries/new-york.

Putnam County Board of Elections. 2015. "Putnam County General Election November 3, 2015." Accessed December 9, 2021. https://putnamboe.com/wp-content/uploads/2015/04/2015-WEBPAGE-ELECTION-RESULTS-CERTIFIED-GENERAL.pdf.

Putnam, Robert D. 2000. *Bowling Alone: The Collapse and Revival of American Community.* New York: Simon & Schuster.

Rensselaer County Legislature. 2019. "2019 Local Laws." Accessed December 11, 2021. https://www.rensselaercounty.org/wp-content/uploads/2019-Local-Laws-1.pdf.

Reynolds, David. 2000. "Third Party Time: How and Why Progressives Are Building a Political Movement." *New Political Science* 22 (2): 177–199.

Rich, Wilbur C. 2007. *David Dinkins and New York City Politics: Race, Images, and the Media.* Albany: State University of New York Press.

Rockland Coalition to End the New Jim Crow. n.d. "About." Accessed December 17, 2021. https://www.facebook.com/EndTheNewJimCrow.

Rockland County Board of Elections. 2018. "Primary Election Results by Race— September 13, 2018." Accessed December 9, 2021. https://rocklandgov.com/departments/board-of-elections/election-results/primary-election-reports-by-race-september-13-2018/.

Rockland United. n.d. "We Are Rockland United." Accessed December 17, 2021. https://rocklandunited.org/.

Roff, Jessica. 2019. "Catskill Community Power Stops Wheelabrator's Toxic Plan." Accessed December 13, 2021. https://www.riverkeeper.org/blogs/ecology/catskill-community-power-stops-wheelabrators-toxic-plan/.

Rom, Gabriel. 2016. "Locals Organize Travel to Women's March on Washington." *Journal News*, December 12, 2012. http://www.lohud.com/story/news/politics/2016/12/12/womens-march-travel/95334048/.

Roscoe, Douglas D., and Shannon Jenkins. 2016. *Local Party Organizations in the Twenty-First Century*. Albany: State University of New York Press.

RUPCO. 2019. "Community Development." Accessed December 16, 2021. https://rupco.org/portfolio-2/community-development/.

SAM Party v. Kosinski. 483 F. Supp. 3d 245, 2020 U.S. Dist. LEXIS 159287, 2020 WL 5359640 (S.D.N.Y., Sept. 1, 2020).

Sanjek, Roger. 2000. *The Future of Us All: Race and Neighborhood Politics in New York City*. Ithaca, NY: Cornell University Press.

Schevtchuk Armstrong, Liz. 2017. "Philipstown Forbids Aiding Immigration Arrests." *Highlands Current*, April 14, 2017. https://highlandscurrent.org/2017/04/14/philipstown-forbids-aiding-immigration-arrests/.

Schneider, Aliya. 2020. "Johnson Signs Law Regulation Short-Term Rentals." Accessed December 12, 2021. https://www.hudsonvalley360.com/news/columbiacounty/johnson-signs-law-regulating-short-term-rentals/article_119072ae-b87d-52ef-956e-e95d28aae003.html.

Schneider, Aliya. 2021. "Working Families Candidates Challenged." Accessed December 7, 2021. https://www.hudsonvalley360.com/news/columbiacounty/working-families-candidates-challenged/article_977cc116-4e7a-51f1-82b3-41b764092600.html.

Schuyler, David. 2018. *Embattled River: The Hudson and Modern American Environmentalism*. Ithaca, NY: Cornell University Press.

Sierra Club New Jersey Chapter. n.d. "Pilgrim Pipeline." Accessed December 11, 2021. https://www.sierraclub.org/new-jersey/pilgrim-pipeline.

Shaheen, Jeanne. 2021. "Heeding Shaheen's Call, FERC Establishes Office to Boost Public Participation at Agency: U.S. Senator Jeanne Shaheen of New Hampshire." Accessed August 13, 2024. https://www.shaheen.senate.gov/news/press/heeding-shaheens-call-ferc-establishes-office-to-boost-public-participation-at-agency.

Skocpol, Theda, and Vanessa Williamson. 2016. *The Tea Party and the Remaking of Republican Conservatism*. New York: Oxford University Press.

Soyer, Daniel. 2012. "'Support the Fair Deal in the Nation; Abolish the Raw Deal in the City': The Liberal Party in 1949." *New York History* 93, no. 2 (Spring):147–181.

Soyer, Daniel. 2022. *Left in the Center: The Liberal Party of New York and the Rise and Fall of American Social Democracy*. Ithaca, NY: Cornell University Press.

Swing Left. n.d. "About Swing Left." Accessed December 19, 2021. https://swingleft.org/about.

Swing Left. n.d.a. "Local Groups." Accessed December 19, 2021. https://swingleft.org/groups.

Terrie, Philip G. 1994. *Forever Wild: A Cultural History of Wilderness in the Adirondacks*. Syracuse, NY: Syracuse University Press.

Town of Tuxedo. 2019. "Climate Smart Community Task Force Pledge." Accessed December 11, 2021. https://www.tuxedogov.org/climate-smart-community-task-force/pages/climate-smart-community-task-force-pledge.

UlsterCorps. 2009. "Second Anniversary Celebration for Save Them Now." Accessed December 16, 2021. https://www.ulstercorps.org/second-anniversary-celebration-for-save-them-now-228/.

Ulster County. 2019. "Ulster County Executive Pat Ryan Signs 'Term Limits' Legislation." Accessed October 3, 2021. https://ulstercountyny.gov/news/executive/ulster-county-executive-pat-ryan-signs-"term-limits"-legislation.

Ulster County Board of Elections. 2002. "Ulster County Official Primary Results for September 10, 2002." Accessed May 1, 2017. http://ulstercountyny.gov/sites/default/files/documents/2002-Primary-Election-Results.pdf.

Ulster County Board of Elections. 2006. "Ulster County Official Election Results for November 7, 2006." Accessed December 12, 2021. https://elections.ulstercountyny.gov/wp-content/uploads/2019/09/2006GeneralElectionResults.pdf.

Ulster County Board of Elections. 2016. "Primary Results." Accessed May 1, 2017. http://ulstercountyny.gov/sites/default/files/primary%20results.pdf.

Ulster County Legislature. 2015. "Resolution No. 38 Opposing the Pilgrim Pipeline." Accessed December 11, 2021. https://legislature.ulstercountyny.gov/sites/default/files/38-15_1.pdf.

United States Census Bureau. 2012. "New York: 2010 Population and Housing Unit Counts." Accessed December 19, 2021. https://www.census.gov/prod/cen2010/cph-2-34.pdf.

United States Census Bureau. 2020. "QuickFacts." Accessed December 22, 2021. https://www.census.gov/quickfacts/fact/table/US/PST045221.

United States Census Bureau. 2021. "Explore Census Data." Accessed December 22, 2021. https://data.census.gov/cedsci/.

United States Election Atlas. 2014. "2014 Gubernatorial Democratic Primary Election Results." Accessed June 6, 2017. https://uselectionatlas.org/RESULTS/state.php?fips=36&year=2014&f=0&off=5&elect=1.

Weigold, Marilyn E., and Yonkers Historical Society. 2014. *Yonkers in the Twentieth Century*. Albany: State University of New York Press.

Welber, Bobby. 2015. "Which Hudson Valley Town Has the Most Liberals?" *Hudson Valley Post*, December 22, 2015. http://hudsonvalleypost.com/which-hudson-valley-town-has-the-most-liberals/.

Willard, Lucas. 2019. "Coeymans Approves Clean Air Law." WAMC, March 29, 2019. https://www.wamc.org/new-york-news/2019-03-29/coeymans-approves-clean-air-law.

Wolfe, Allen. 1968. "The Withering Away of the American Labor Party." *Journal of the Rutgers University Library* 31 (2): 46–57.

Working Families Party. 2017. "Apply for the New York WFP Endorsement." Last modified July 1, 2017. http://workingfamilies.org/endorsement/new-york/apply-wfp-endorsement/.

Index

www.ingramcontent.com/pod-product-compliance
Lightning Source LLC
Chambersburg PA
CBHW050712280326
41926CB00088B/3003